Heavenly Bodies and

Other Diversions

Nathaniel Robert Winters

Nathaniel R. Winters

BUFFALO PRINTINGCOMPANY

Napa Valley California

Cover art photo by Frank Leonard

Cover art NGC3603 from NASA, ESA Hubble collaboration

ACKNOWLEDGEMNTS

I owe my writing chops to many and I want to acknowledge and thank them.

First off to my major muse and favorite heavenly body, my wife, Colleen.

To the Thursday morning Solstices Writers who have brought poetry and some beauty and insanity into my life.

To Ana Manwaring and the countless number of writers who have shared critiques and their work with me.

To the Redwood and Napa branches of the California Writers Club.

To Cathy Carsell, editor, proof reader, and helper.

To my friends and family, thank you for your help.

And a thank you to all the heavenly bodies near and far that inspire and stimulate my imagination.

Thanks to you all.

Table of Contents

1. Heavenly Bodies and Other Diversions   7
2. Parkinson's Disease and Other Diversions   8
3. Dr. Seuss Affliction Prescription   10
4. It Makes No Sense   12
5. Me   13
6. The Other Side of Me   14
7. Pre-Dawn Positano   16
8. Caesar-Land   17
9. Dangerous Curves   19
10. Playing in Heaven   35
11. Lunch with Lucas   36
12. Restoration   38
13. Choosing Crossroads   40
14. Fishing for a Legend   41
15. Late Night Jitterbug   50
16. No Place for a Wallflower   51
17. Ode to a Veteran   53
18. Omaha Beach   57
19. Rumors About My Father   60
20. Saturday Morning Heroes   64

21. First Kiss	66
22. Finding Shelter From the Cold	72
23. Still Finding Shelter From the Cold	79
24. Past the Future	80
25. Friday the Fourteenth	86
26. High Holy Daze Dream	93
27. Another High Holy Daze Dream	95
28. The Round Trip	97
29. The Rick Hegner Story	108
30. A Double Agent	114
31. The Other Band of Brothers	116
32. A True War Hero	138
33. Finding Colleen	140
34. Rock and Roll	145
35. Goodbye to The Stick	148
36. The October Invasion	151
37. Land of the Giants	152
38. Who That Foe From	153
39. Goodbye Too Soon	154
40. Golden Record	155

41. The Runaway   157

42. Man in the Shadows   167

43. Past Times   169

44. Wine Country Fires   170

45. Mother Nature's Plan   171

46. Thicker Than Smoke   173

47. Another West Side Story 175

48. A Different View   178

49. Classic Classical Rock   180

50. Jefferson's Confession   181

51. Driving Her Crazy   183

52. Ghosts of Abbott and Costello 186

53. Once Upon a Time   190

Heavenly Bodies and Other Diversions

I feel a magnetic attraction to heavenly bodies

both on earth and out in the universe

attraction that drives to distraction

with a galaxy of star's significance

One body was unique

a mystery with long history

powerful pull of a black hole

once entrapped, no way out

No rocket had the thrust

to find a way to freedom

trapped by an infinite force field

of her heavenly body's gravity

Parkinson's Disease, the not so Heavenly Other Diversion

I was diagnosed with Parkinson's Disease in 2007 just after two unsuccessful back surgeries. Now I figure the Parkinson's could have instigated the back problems in the first place and maybe the lack of success of the attempted two operational fixes.

Many have asked me, "What is Parkinson's disease and how has it affected your life?"

Allow me to fill you in:

Parkinson's disease attacks one's nervous system and brain. Most notably, the part of the brain that makes the hormone dopamine. As the body starts to lack this chemical, movement is affected. At first one part on one side starts to shake. With me it was my left pinky. That is how I was first diagnosed.

I was told, "The disease is a nervous disorder that continually progresses and there is no cure. How fast it progresses is different in each patient. The major drug taken to stem the effects of the disease is synthesized dopamine."

I have had to take more of the medication as the Parkinson's progresses. Also, I have had DBS (Brian surgery) to counter shaking and stiffness.

How am I affected?

Let me count the ways:

1. muscle stiffness which along with my back problem makes it hard to sit

2. shaking

3. loss of smell

4. constipation

5. with combined back problem, no tennis, skiing, or running

6. some memory loss

7. dyskinesia (head jerking)

8. depression

9. anxiety

10. driving restrictions

So, how do I deal with all of this?

For the most part, I'm okay.

Every sunrise is a new day.

Importantly, Rue, my dog, walks with me, a mile each morning through grapevines to the Napa River and back; looking up at hills filled with redwood forest.

I take and teach writing classes, tutor and write almost every day.

Each day is a special gift, shared with my wife, my son and friends.

Dr. Seuss Affliction Prescription

Home from the pain clinic for Thanksgiving,

I had learned the skills to start re-living.

Had been away for six long weeks

gave mind and body much needed tweaks.

Skiing and tennis were gone, happily life goes on.

Early retirement and a little pain were not so bad,

I knew good times could still be had.

I was completely free to be what was left of me.

With a little pain I could walk a mile,

or write a story to make people smile.

In a good chair that fit,

If not too long, I could sit.

Not having to answer the school bell,

I had the time for a story to tell.

Then just a few weeks later,

I found my world did crater.

Reaching to close a door,

A very simple task,

I've done a million times before,

I noticed something strange, my pinkie shook.

I shut my eyes, tried again, then took another look.

Yes, it did, it shook even when I reached for a book.

"Tisk, task," I said, it's no big deal,"

nothing serious, I really did feel.

The doctor said, "I don't want to make you pout,

you need to find out what this is about."

So off I went no time to flee,

to the clinic, the neurologist I did see.

The specialist put me through each and every test

and I tried so hard to do my very best.

Finally she told me, yes she did,

something that couldn't be hid.

I never heard these words before.

"You have Parkinson's disease, there is no cure.

The disease it is progressive, you will get worse,

it doesn't kill, so no need to call a hearse."

My mind got foggy, her voice far away,

sat, tried to listen, there I had to stay.

So now I take dopamine my body does crave,

keeps me from shaking like an ocean wave.

I learned the way; two pills five times a day.

You do see I stay quite busy,

and use walking sticks when I get dizzy.

It's mostly okay with the medication,

last year I even went on a vacation.

But please excuse me, try to relate,

if to my destination I'm a little bit late.

December 2013
IT MAKES NO SENSE

Rich pitchy aroma of pine burning,

always smelled heavenly, divine,

until Parkinson's, you might know,

robbed me the use of that nose of mine.

That's right, my sniffer can't smell

to tell good wine from bad in a snifter.

So, you may silently fart in the car I don't mind,

whatever comes out of your behind is benign.

August on the N.Y. subway's no sweat

Even if the guy next to me's tee shirts all wet.

Baby's diaper change, I do not fear,

what the heck I'll volunteer.

Cutting onions, not a problem,

it doesn't raise a tear.

The worst garlic breath

won't send me away

and if there's a dead skunk,

just show me the way.

But I think I would really mind

 if I go blind.

ME

I cry at movies when they're sad
happy ones too unless their bad
in touch with my feminine side
but male domination I can't hide

Love sports, even macho football,
baseball, hoops, soccer, tennis, all,
not golf, "A good walk ruined." (Will Rogers)
eighteen holes can't end too soon

Love to read or write a good book
I've written quite a few, take a look
still a student and teacher
with my son, never a preacher

Always loved history
its stories never a mystery
love for the great outdoors
in nature always wanting more

Like to think I'm a renaissance man
Da Vinci and Jefferson, I'm a fan
so, I guess this is me
it's all I ever wanted to be

The Other Side of Me

Sometimes I find myself in a really bad mood
when I just want to stay home and brood
Parkinson's symptoms abound
dark clouds follow me around

Out for my walk the last two weeks
two friendly dogs knocked me off my feet
now my shoulder and knee
join my back to torture me

I went with friends to a ballet show
about a man with Parkinson's I did not know
his wife and daughter danced while he progressed
then the man died, leaving me depressed

My wife goes out in the sunshine to play
while I'm left home all alone to stay
I want her to enjoy tennis and have fun
but I can no longer hit the ball and run

So, I write another story or poem

something I can enjoy at home

yet, I miss playing games with a ball

or skiing down a mountain as snow falls

So, you see, the other side of me

Pre-dawn Positano, Italy 2013

Early morning light touches me like a lover away too long.
Blue-grey sea lies flat, becalmed after a week of churning
turbulence.

Clouds hide the rising sun dulling pastel walls, terracotta roofs.
Hotels, houses hang precariously from eroding limestone
cliffs.

The black sand and pebble beach
enriched by Vesuvius' volcanic eruptions two centuries earlier
looks up with waves that wink and smile.
"Come play with me," she says seductively.
I answer, "Be patient, it's early. I'm in no hurry.
I'll explore your offerings slowly, like wine that grows from your
hillsides."

Positano; small quiet-refuge from invading barbarian hordes.
No "Pax-Romana" in treasure trove modern Italy.
Like Goths, Visigoths and Huns, torrents of tourists sack,
plunder cities.
Impossible to saver anything of value or beauty,
as multitudes compete like gladiators before every historical
wonder.

Transition from night to day—almost complete.Looking down
at the beautiful beckoning Mediterranean Sea, I take a breath.
Pause to reflect and recognize gifts of genius Italian ancestors
offered to the world.

Caesar-land

Reflections on Rome or What I Learned from Uncle Walt

I loved visiting Rome but could not avoid thinking that it was too much Roman Catholic and not enough Ancient Rome. I wanted to see more history. The Coliseum and the Forum were cool but just wetted my appetite.

I want to present an alternative to the typical Rome Vatican trip. Not that the Pope's place wasn't amazing and let's let the Church pull in tourists and make some money. That artwork is truly astonishing. But I want more Roman Empire stuff.

OK, so here is my proposal, drum roll please: CAESAR-LAND a place to make Ancient Rome come alive:

1. The Roman Coliseum refurbished with
   A. Gladiator fights (Ok it's the 21 century no killing)
   B. Chariot Races
   C. Olympic style sporting events (I Know that was Greek but - close enough.)

2. Roman Forum-land with recreated scenes from history like Julius Caesar being stabbed.

3. Roman legion battles including Rome vs. Carthage complete with Hannibal's Elephants (See A- no killing please)

4. A real Roman orgy (adults only)

5. Plundering - A visit to the Roman shopping district.

6. We end the program day with the Vesuvius mountain fireworks spectacular.

You think this is really a stupid idea, don't you?

Really?

Think about all the money Disneyland and Disneyworld rakes-in. Anything that brings history alive is Ok with me.

After all I went to Rome to praise Caesar not to bury him.

The following short story won a Jessamyn West award for fiction:

Dangerous Curves

She walked into my office on a Friday, I remember because I planned to play in my weekly poker game. I never got to that poker game because that lady got to me.

She was dressed to kill, short black dress with a string of pearls falling into a deep dark valley of cleavage. Her body filled the tiny dress like a straight flush, with more dangerous curves than Highway 1 at Big Sur. Long sheer nylon covered legs ending in black stilettos, almost making her as tall as my six feet two.

She brushed back wisps of brown hair from an angelic face with eyes bluer then tropical Pacific waters. Yet something in those eyes told me she was no angel.

"You're Chad Powers, private detective, right? I googled your name and address, mostly four and five-star reviews; I'm impressed."

I got up from my desk and came around to greet her. "And you are?" I put out my paw.

She tried to smile as her fingers found my hand, "Lucy Rogers," she said.

"Well Mrs. Rogers, what can I do for you?"

"That's Miss Rogers, Lucy. Please call me Lucy. Someone. . . Someone is trying to kill me."

I pointed to the chair. "Please sit-down Lucy and fill me in."

Her blue eyes tinged with red, I assumed from tears.

She said, "I was driving to my home in the Berkeley hills two nights ago when my car stalled and wouldn't start. Only two blocks from my house, I decided to walk. Tires screeched and a car bore down on me. Desperate, I dove behind a parked car barely escaping. The car did a three-point turn and came at me again. It veered off as I was able to move behind a big eucalyptus tree by the sidewalk. I dialed 911; never so scared in all my life."

"Fifteen minutes later the police arrived. I gave them my statement but they said 'there was not much to go on; if you see that car again, call.' That's when shock hit me and I broke down and cried."

"Do you know what type of car it was?"

"No idea, it was white and had headlights. Maybe it was one of those big old American cars. The next day, I took my car to

the repair shop, they told me somebody put water in the gas tank. Mr. Powers. Do you think you can help me?"

"Sure Lucy, we'll treat this the same way I would've dealt with a murder case when I was a police detective. We need to find means, motive, and opportunity. Let's start with the basics. Who would want to hurt you?"

"I have no idea."

"Boyfriend?"

"I guess the way I would put it is, I'm taking a break from relationships."

"Old boyfriend?"

"Jerry? No, he's a pussycat and we're still friends."

I was really liking the idea of spending time with a single Miss Lucy and tracking down her assailant. "I'm afraid this might take some time. Let's go get some dinner and you try to think of anybody that my want to do this to you."

At dinner she filled in some of the blanks about of her life. The 27-year-old Miss Rogers had worked for an East Bay high-tech startup but took a leave of absence to help her dad who

was dying of cancer. Her mom died in a car accident, two years earlier. Her younger sister had a past drug problem and was a single mom.

When I brought up the sister as a suspect, Lucy totally ruled her out. "Are you kidding, my sister loves me."

Sorry Lucy, I thought to myself your sister is the most obvious candidate. I didn't tell her.

I knew it broke all my rules about work and play but the attraction was electric. She flirted like she might also be feeling the high voltage.

I followed her home to check out the location of the car attack and make sure she was safe. When we got to her house she was actually shaking. She said, "I'm scared; will you stay with me?"

I couldn't say no to a damsel in distress. Suddenly she was in my arms and my rules about mixing romance and work flew out the window like a murder of crows. It sure beat a night playing poker.

In the morning I woke early. Lucy's blue eyes were still closed. I hated to wake sleeping beauty but before I started my investigation I had to make sure this lovely lady was somewhere safe.

"Lucy rise and shine darlin'. I have work to do. Pack a bag, leave your car. I'll take you to the train station; you need to get

out of town for a few days. Go to Reno, play some slots. I'd rather you gamble with your money than your life.

I kept an eye on the rear view to make sure we weren't followed to the station.

On the platform, she kissed my cheek. I watched as she walked away to get on the train, hips swaying naturally.

Damn, I thought, no one should look that good. Back in the car, I wiped the blood-red lipstick off my face and tried to forget last night.

Playing with a client usually meant trouble.

***

I started with the pussycat, old boyfriend Jerry. I had a hard time believing it was that easy to let Lucy go. Dead end, he was out of town during the car incident.

So, I checked out the sister. Finding her house was easy enough, almost too easy

these days with GPS. It used to take some work to find things, now any idiot with a smartphone can find anybody. Technology; it's here, so I use it.

Tina Rogers had a three-bedroom rental house in south Berkeley. Not the best neighborhood but not the worst either. An older green Toyota sat in the driveway. I wasn't planning a major stake out, just wanted to watch the place for an hour that Saturday morning. I was still reading the Chronicle sports section when Tina came out with her three-year-old son, who Lisa told me was Danny.

Tina was an okay looking young woman with bleached blond hair and a cute face but she was no Lucy. I've seen this dynamic before--call it the younger sibling syndrome. Don't know if the shrinks actually have a name for it—when the younger sister is compared to the older and can't quite make the grade. They just give up or rebel. You've seen it haven't you? Makes me glad I was an only child.

Tina and Danny got in her car and drove away. Thought I knew where they were going, Lucy insisted that she call and tell her sister she had to go out of town. So, Tina would look in on their dad at the nursing home; played a hunch and followed her anyway. Tina entered the freeway going south towards Oakland, not the direction of the nursing home. This might get interesting.

Insurance companies pay good money to find fraud dead beats. Most private cases usually involve working for husbands cheating on their wives or wives cheating on their husbands. A camera would be more useful than a weapon, so I normally don't take a gun.

I've never had a case where somebody told me that someone was trying to kill them, so I was packing my old '38 service revolver.

Tina exited the freeway south of downtown and pulled up to a rickety, paint peeling mess of a house in a gang infested neighborhood. My un-dented two-year old red Honda stood out like a cat at a dog show and knew if I stayed here long my cover would be blown.

I slowed down just enough to see an old white, bald tire, Ford, the type that I would have driven as a police detective. Could this be the assault vehicle?

Rolling slowly, I grabbed my camera and took a video of Tina and the four men she joined out front before they retreated into the house.

My Honda continued until I found myself in front of the downtown police station; still had friends on the force from before the lawsuit.

Chuck Mills had been working a gang and drug task force; one look at the video and he laughed.

"You have some bad characters here." He ran the plates on the Ford. It belonged to slick Andy Simmons. "Andy is a major drug dealer, including meth and heroin, his rap sheet includes assault with a deadly weapon, drug dealing and vehicular homicide."

"Bingo, you just said the magic words, thanks."

I tried to figure out how to give Lucy the bad news about her sister.

The morning had been clear and the bright sun reflected off the bay but the summer fog was coming in. I could see it clawing at the Golden Gate Bridge as I scooted back to Berkeley.

Let's go see how the girl's father's doing. I googled Thomas Rogers on my hands-free device during the ride.

He was a self-made millionaire in the post war plastics industry. Maybe that obnoxious guy at the pool party in the movie The Graduate was right. I chuckled to myself, "Plastics,"

26

and stopped to scarf down some Pad Thai before visiting the care home.

An aide took me to see Thomas Rogers. His appearance led me to believe that the grim reaper was swinging in the on-

deck circle. In spite of the danger, with her father so sick, I knew I had to get Lucy back home.

Cell phone in hand I called.

"Hello," Lucy answered.

I filled her in on the latest developments.

She said, "My sister? No, I refuse to believe it."

I tread carefully, "I'm just giving the facts, no opinion. I wish it were different." In spite of myself I heard me saying, "Maybe you're in denial? It's not just a river in Egypt, you know." I regretted saying that as soon as I heard it come out my mouth.

She said coldly, "I think not."

"Lucy, I didn't say that to be mean but to wake you up. Remember someone is trying to kill you."

I could almost feel her anger through the phone. "Okay, but I need to talk to her, you can come with me. I'll take the next plane to Oakland and call with the details."

"Sounds like a plan. I'll meet your plane."

She took a deep sigh, "Bye." Click.

***

Two hours later I watched her plane land in Oakland. Lucy didn't exactly run into my arms. The purveyor of bad news often takes the blame. She did not like me fingering her sister.

The Sharks Hockey Team could have played on the ice between us. No hello, thanks for meeting me; oh well, all part of the job. I just hoped I could keep her safe.

"You didn't call her?" I asked.

"No, but I'm trying to add up the numbers. Even if I multiply, I don't get ten. Tina has never shown me any hostility, murder no way."

"Okay, I'm playing it your way. Let's go talk to her."

As we drove to Berkeley I tried to break the icicles. "How was Reno?"

Her cold blue eyes bore into me, and notorious chilly foggy bay winds arrived on the east side of the bay. My leather jacket held no warmth. I blasted the heat in the Honda during the strangely silent drive.

When we pulled up to Tina's house, I noticed only the Toyota. Relived, I still watched hawk—like as we closed in on the front door.

The moment I saw them together I knew I was wrong. I saw smiles then hugs. Danny came shouting, "Aunty!"

Nephew tucked in her arms, Lucy gave me a, you're crazy look.

I shrugged my shoulders, "So I'm wrong." I smiled at her happiness.

Still my detective nose smelled a rat and my bet, he was in this house today.

"Lucy, I've still got to ask Tina some questions."

Lucy's happiness bubble burst. "Tina," she said, "this is Chad Powers." She proceeded to fill her sister in.

It was time I did my detective thing. "Tina please remember your sister's life is on the line. Do you know Andy Simmons?"

"Of course, he's Danny's father."

"You know he's been arrested by the police before?"

Nathaniel R. Winters

"Well, Yeah."

"Did you see him today?"

"Yeah."

"He's been arrested for manslaughter and assault with a deadly weapon."

"You know, we haven't been together much since Danny was born."

I leaned in, "Does he have a white full-size Ford?"

"Yeah."

"Why did you see him today?" I asked.

Tina squirmed in her seat. "Well he has been so nice lately. We are actually married you know. He's been talking about getting back together."

I looked at Lucy, her mouth dropped open in surprise and those blue eyes went from her sister to me with a knowing look.

I said, "It looks like all the cards have been dealt. We've found our motive. You have a very wealthy father, who is about to

30

die. I'm sorry if I'm being insensitive, but we have more important things to worry about, like your malicious husband.

Suddenly he wants you back and if he could do away with your sister—well it's twice the money."

Tina burst into tears. Lucy had a new look in her eyes, they almost smiled while the rest of her face wore a frown.

"He's waiting for you out there--for both of you," I said, "He's not here but he knows where both of you live. But he doesn't know about me. That's our ace in the hole."

Tina, call him, say you want a divorce and tell him you will be staying with your sister. Lucy, we'll switch cars and today you park on the street and tonight I'll park in your drive. My bet-- he'll make his move tonight and I'll be waiting when he breaks in." I'll be there before dark, I just want to check on some things."

"What if he comes during the day?" Lucy asked.

"I don't think he would take that chance, but do you have a gun?"

"No, I've never felt comfortable having one in the house."

"Take mine just in case he shows up. But don't get trigger happy and shoot him. Just hold him and call me."

As I made the last turn to Lucy's house, I saw the white Ford on the street. Andy got there before me—damn it! Just then— POW! I heard a gunshot. I beelined to open the front door and flew in gun in hand. Lucy stood there with my '38 pointed at me and a wicked smile on her face.

"Drop it, she demanded."

I tossed my gun down on the blood stained oriental rug, where Andy lay, hole in his chest, river of red pouring out.

"Thank you for the use of your gun. I will make it look like he broke in, you shot him and he plugged you. That's one less person I have to worry about getting my father's money. And Mr. Powers, as much as I enjoyed your...a...company...it will get rid of you, too—the only witness."

"What about your sister?" I asked.

"That druggy. I convinced her it would be a good idea to have a drink or two. The worthless bitch is passed out upstairs. So much for her two years clean." She laughed. "I can inject an overdose later."

I shook my head. "And your nephew?"

"He's at the baby sitter's. Don't you think he'll look good in a military school uniform? Now it's time to say goodbye, Chad."

It was my turn to smile. "Joe, the front door's open."

Three policeman appeared guns drawn.

"Put the weapon down!" The Sargent demanded.

"Lucy, do you know what night it is? It's Friday, my poker night. It appears I have a stronger hand, three of a kind beats

a queen of hearts even with your ace in the hole. Your hand is busted."

"Here is her confession, Joe" I took my phone from my pocket.

"You never read me my rights." Lucy said.

"I don't have to read you any rights my dear, I'm a P.I. Not a cop anymore."

"What…how…did you know?" The lady stammered.

"Two tells that gave your hand away, the first—I noticed your eyes smile at Tina's despair. The second; when you said you didn't have a gun in your house. The night I stayed over I noticed a rifle in your bedroom closet."

"I ran your record at the station. It seems you shot an old boyfriend and got off for self-defense."

"Joe," I said to my card playing buddy, "read the lady her rights and be careful. She plays a killer game of poker and cheats when no one's looking."

I was careful driving down the hill with its dangerous curves and the cold bay fog blowing in. I felt a chill. Was it the fog or remembering Lucy's icy blue eyes?

She was the kind of girl that made my Uncle Sidney say to me, "Dames; you can't live with 'em and you're not allowed to shoot 'em." I sighed, shook my head and turned up the heat.

PLAYING IN HEAVEN

My dream drifted back fifteen years

to powdered white winter

at the top of the world.

Lake Tahoe winked

one deep blue eye at me.

Turned skis downhill

played in heaven

floated atop

puffy cumulus clouds

then down through

evergreen alpine trees

laughing at every turn

my mountain winter wonderland

Lunch with Lucas

George checked out of Modesto shortly after graduating from Davis High. But something very cool from *American Graffiti* was left behind. Over near Five Corners in old downtown, on G-Street where teens in cars still cruised 'til their personal curfew, stood a real A&W *Happy Days* style car hop.

Cute waitresses dressed in shorts and tees still skated over to take orders as Rock & Roll blasted from your car speakers. One of the girls took my order. About ten minutes later she skated over with my lunch and attached those silly trays to my car window. In a bag on top was a Big Boy type of cheeseburger, French fries and of course, a gigantic mug containing an ice-cold root beer float. All for a few bucks, including a nice tip for the skating queen waitress.

Just another hundred-degree summer's day in Modesto.

The only thing missing was my old 57 Chevy from back in my high school days. Was that Ron Howard and George Lucas over in the car next to me? No, it couldn't be. But it sure looked like them.

Restoration

To the new Bay Bridge, I toast
to the new spans beauty we can boast
More famous is the Golden Gate
but the new Bay Bridge is at least as great

New span looks so fine
with east sides sexy new lines
looking at both from a high ridge
I vote for the pretty new bridge

It carries more people every day
from east to west the best way
BART is fine if you're going downtown
but to too many places it's not around

When the old bridge fell from the quake
far too long the positions did take
debating design and cost
way too much time was lost

But they finally got it right

after all the years fight

of the new span we can be proud

restoring the way we get around

Choosing Crossroads

Which way to heaven and hell?

Do you think you always can tell?

Or does good and evil both lie inside

Like Stevenson's Dr. Jekyll and Mr. Hyde?

Does the Devil make us do it?

Or do we have free will to choose it?

How could Thomas Jefferson proclaim,

All men are created the same

with certain inalienable rights,

while he worked slaves days and nights?

Did God reside

on the Allies' side

defeating Nazis, saving Jews?

but not when Custer butchered the Sioux?

At crossroads of right and wrong

we must make choices all along

 only your conscience might know

which is righteous way to go

Fishing for a Legend

Lisa Collins and her younger sister met Papa Hemingway, who was between wives, just before the Second World War. Lisa was awed by his presence, having read many of his books and stories. She thought he was so brutally handsome, holding court in a backwater Cuban honky-tonk, like he owned the place, which he did.

He sent the women two Cuba Libras and asked, "What's a nice couple of young Yankee girls doing in a dive like this?"

"Actually, we were looking for you," Lisa said, a sly smile on her face.

Hemingway was with two of his friends and they slinked to the girl's table like lions stalking prey. "These two gentlemen are good friends, Philipe, from the former Spanish Republic and Pepe is from right here in Havana."

The pretty brunette, said, "I'm Lisa and this is my younger sister Kate. We are from Pennsylvania."

Her sister was blond, buxom, gorgeous and more than a little star struck. Lisa could tell because she too was a little bit blinded by the glow of this literary star. She had been a literature major at the University of Pennsylvania and studied the already legendary author. She heard the vagabond frequented this bar and set off to find him.

Lisa said, "I studied you in college and I was hoping to write my master's thesis about you."

"I'm flattered," Hemingway said.

"We wanted to go to Paris but with war threatening we decided to come to Havana, soak up some sun and look for you." Lisa said.

"You are unescorted?" Ernest asked.

"Our father is a train conductor. He had to work so he was not able to come. After our mother died in a car accident three years ago, Dad tends to indulge his girls but he trusts us. We are quite capable to escort each other."

He shook his head like he didn't approve, then just shrugged. "How would you like to go fishing tomorrow?"

Kate who jumped at the prospect said, "Oh Lisa, I want to go."

Lisa's face lit up. "Thank you that would be very nice but can we trust you? You have a notorious reputation," she said, a flirting smile teasing the man.

"I promise to be on my best behavior," he said smiling holding up three fingers like a boy scout. "Can you be ready at nine a.m.?"

"All right Mr. Hemingway we will be ready at nine."

"Good, call me Papa please. Pepe will pick you up at your hotel."

They all finished their drinks and the girls departed.

When they were far away enough for privacy, Lisa did a little jig of happiness. "Holy Toledo! I can't believe we are going fishing with Papa Hemingway."

***

The excited girls awoke at dawn.

Kate asked, "What should we wear?"

They had both worn long flowing flower print wrap around skirts and sleeveless blouses the night before.

Lisa took charge. "We might want to swim so we will wear our bathing suits under our clothing. I'm going with blue shorts and red top. How 'bout you put on the cute navy outfit, white and blue. Red scarf for me and blue for you. Bring an extra outfit in case we get soaked.'"

Kate said, "Check and check," then jumped into her clothing. She walked into her sprayed perfume mist, applied some lipstick, a touch of ruse and said, ready.

Lisa taking a bit longer applying eye shadow, looked over at her sister the blond bombshell and just shook her head. "Yup, you're ready. It takes me twice as long to look half as good as you."

Kate giggled, "Yes, I guess you got the brain and I got the bosom. But sis, you look darn good in your new bathing suit."

"Well, don't forget to take the bug spray and I'll meet you downstairs for breakfast."

Each girl ate a full breakfast; eggs, toast and lots of rich Cuban coffee con leche on the hotel veranda. They were still there sipping the liquid from locally grown beans when Pepe arrived in an old pickup truck. He left the engine running and jumped out to help gather the girls and their things.

Hemingway greeted the girls at the pier, "Good morning. Don't you ladies look lovely. Ready to catch some fish?"

"Hi Papa," The sisters called out almost in unison.

They kissed European style touching cheeks on each side.

"She's all ready to go Papa," Philipe said in perfect English, his Castilian accent sounding exotic to the girls.

"Hop on girls and choose a side." Ernest said.

There were four fishing chairs. The women grabbed two, port side.

Hemingway took the wheel and shouted, "Away all lines. Pepe and Philipe untied the boat and jumped on. The big diesel engine growled to life and black smoke billowed from the rear as they backed out. Ernest pushed the control sticks forward and the boat took off into the Caribbean.

The boat skipped along the waves. The sea sparkled in sunshine and the weather was calm, a perfect day for fishing. When they reached a favorite spot, Ernest cut the engine, dropped anchor, and joined the girls.

Pepe and Philipe prepared the rods, reels, bait and tackle. Ernest joined the women, showed Kate how to cast the big weighted line into the sea and gave her the rod.

"If you get a hit, just hand the line to me and I'll take care of the rest." Earnest suggested.

Lisa pulled up a deck chair next to Ernest and took out her notebook to interview the writer for her thesis.

The Spaniard and his Cuban amigo had all the luck pulling in a few good-sized fish. They grilled them for lunch, Cuban style, the smell caused the girls mouths to water.

After lunch all five went for a swim and Kate flirted innocently with Philipe splashing him with waves then swimming away laughing.

Back on-board Lisa continued her interview under some shade while Ernest and Kate fished in the hot sun.

Kate took a break. All the men's eyes turned to her as she rubbed lotion on her body and laid in the shade.

Papa put down his tackle to join the young blond. Meanwhile Lisa took a turn in Earnest's chair when…wham! She got a strike.

She screeched, "Help! What do I do?"

Ernest couldn't take the rig and get back in the chair without losing the fish. So, it was up to Lisa and she got to work. Papa sat in the other chair and coached Lisa during the battle.

"Catching a fish is like starting a love affair. You need to feel when to let him run and when to reel him in. That's a good girl you're doing very well."

Pepe said, as he watched the fish jump, "Wow, she is a beauty."

Lisa braced the pole between her legs. She bent forward reeling in the slack. The huge blue fish jumped again. It looked to be the size of a whale as it splashed back down into the sea.

Lisa and the fish fought like Joe Lewis and Max Schmeling in a title fight. Kate rubbed Lisa's hurting, tired shoulders as she brought the fish closer. For two solid hours the battle raged. Lisa with bulldog tenacity persevered. Pepe and Philipe finally netted the monster. The marlin stretched out in the back of the boat was longer then the boat was wide. It was a magnificent prize.

Ernest was feeling a little jealous. He was a macho man and prided himself as the best at everything. To be beaten by a girl seemed inconceivable.

The girls were tired and sunburned, ready to go in but Ernest insisted he be given one last try to bag a big one himself. After an hour, he pouted and gave in. He pulled up anchor and headed towards his pier.

In the shack, rum filled glasses and the four toasted Lisa's victory. Ernest admitted it was one of the largest fish he had ever seen caught. He suggested she take the marlin to a taxidermist to be mounted.

Lisa said, "All I want is a picture taken with the fish and one with you and my sister and you can have the darn thing."

Hemmingway bowed slightly towards Lisa and said, "Really, you would do that for me. I'm very grateful." His mood immediately changed. "Let's have a party," he declared.

"I'm whipped." Lisa said.

Kate said, "Me too. I'm sunburnt. Please Papa, take us back.'

"All right," he said reluctantly, the girls could see his disappointment.

They arrived back at the hotel and Ernest escorted them to the lobby, then into the bar.

"Drinks for everybody on me," he announced. "This lovely young lady here caught the biggest damn fish I ever did see, all by herself. The day belongs to her."

Kate held up a glass and said, "To my big sister."

Lisa blushed, gave a shy smile and said, "To Papa Hemingway, Viva Cuba!"

**

Lisa wound up getting an "A" on her Master's Thesis. Later she would become a well-known war reporter in the Pacific for the New York Times.

Kate joined the Navy during the war and landed an even bigger fish. She married an admiral.

Late Night Jitterbug

A rose in full bloom so beautiful
ruby lips and cheeks silky smooth
fragrance so intoxicating
no place for a wallflower

Like the flora in a Disney cartoon
this lovely flower moved to music
held the wounded in embrace
a last dance for the dying

She came to me long wilted
pollen played seeds spread
around the countryside
new flowers to behold

She shared with me
the special flavor
of her rosehip tea
brewed carefully, a tasty blend

The previous poem was inspired by World War II veteran Iola Hitt.

She was a spry ninety-two-year-old in 2012 when I met her in my writing class. She asked me to write her story of the war. It was a privilege.

Excerpt from:

No Place for a Wallflower

November 15, 1944   La Havre, France

After five days at sea, we arrived at the port of La Havre, France. It bustled with activity. Soldiers gathered in trucks and moved out almost as fast as they came in.

Swarming, unending lines of Army workers unloaded supplies from cargo ships. Another swarm would reload them onto convoys of trucks. It reminded me of ants on the farm.

Many buildings showed extensive damaged. The rubble moved out of the streets, sat piled high by the sides of the road. Both, the Allies and Germans rained bombs down on this important port. I believed it would take years to make this city whole again.

Called aside by my CO, Major Pam Jenkins. I saluted, "You wanted to see me ma'am."

"Sit down, Lieutenant," she said with a frown on her face. "I wish there was a better time and place to give you this."

She handed me a letter sized piece of paper. I looked at a telegram from Mr. and Mrs. Palmer.

The paper read: "Iola, Bob was shot down over the South Pacific in his B29 and is missing in action. STOP

If we hear anything more we will telegram. STOP"

Western Union charged by the word.

The telegram was so short, so simple and so heartbreaking.

It was dated October 2; had taken that long to catch up with me.

I never did meet Bob's parents.

In some ways, being in the army when you got this kind of news was hard, you could never be alone. I went to my bunk and cried. Word quickly spread around the unit.

In other ways, being in the army when you go this type of news was easier because you had to be alone.

After the war, I thought about him sometimes. I loved him. I guess what happened was fate. After all I had a wonderful marriage.

But every once in a while, I wondered…?

Ode to a Veteran

No big deal, look evil in the face

save the human race

keep black storm from our shore

nothing more

When it was over

never marched in a parade

or wanted a medal

returned to his life,

to find himself a wife

I can't let Veteran's Day

come and go

without remembering

how much we owe

Drove a landing-craft at Casablanca

then at deadly Normandy beach,

front gate opened, eyes did see

thousands fell on shore

or the blood- red sea

After bringing in a second wave

fished wounded from waves

screaming for bandages

or early graves

His little escort joined

a convoy of hope

to bombed out Britain under the gun

and Russia, almost completely over-run

Across the cold Atlantic,

frozen North Sea, no time to dwell

chased by unseen wolf-packs

from depths of hell

Scores of vultures dived from sky,

hot breath of fire, causing thousands to die

if tossed into water death quickly struck

seas frigid fingers made rescue pure luck

Plucky Convoy fought back

firing clouds of "ack-ack"

so many vultures he could not miss

ugly birds fell in a burning hiss

His little ship and others chased

wolf-packs from the seas

depth charged, U-boats 'till

desperate brought to their knees

Let us pause, raise a glass, fly the flag,

gather their planted sweet fruit

 I remember your nightmares, Dad

all toast and salute

Boatswain's Mate First class Leo Winetzky

(Winters) 1914-1999

That was a poem about my father's roll during World War II.

The next piece of prose won an award from the Redwood

Writers Club-- the largest chapter of The California Writers

Club, started by Jack London among others.

Omaha Beach

The sea was an ugly shade of green, tossing the enormous fleet of ships like toys in the bathtub of a boy having a temper tantrum. Leo Winetzky was at home in the surging swells as he maneuvered his landing craft below the transport's netting. The man had been driving boats since as an early teen, during Prohibition, he ferried booze across the Detroit River at night.

A year earlier at the invasion of North Africa he boated troops to Casablanca where the Vichy French waved the white flag shortly after the US Navy opened fire. Assigned to the destroyer escort, USS Patterson, he became a well-seasoned combat veteran. On convoy duty he helped his ship fight off enemy submarines and he shot down attacking Nazi bombers.

The invasion of Normandy had been put off a day because of stormy weather, but the next night, the ships sailed from Britain in the churning North Sea, on their date with destiny.

It was June 6, 1944 when he tossed a line from his landing craft to the sailor on the transport, which was quickly secured, holding the boat against the big ships hull. Twenty-four seasick soldiers climbed down the netting and into his bouncing boat as an awesome naval barrage continued.

Clouds were dissipating and as far as he could see, ships of all types and sizes were lined up behind his boat.

Smoke and shells filled the air and exploded on the French shore. He turned the vessel toward that beach which had been given the code name Omaha. A long line of landing crafts joined him, the first wave. Thousands of Americans were there to begin to take France back from the occupying Nazi hordes.

The seasoned German army was waiting for them behind Hitler's sea wall. Had the Naval barrage softened the defenses enough, Leo wondered anxiously?

The answer came suddenly and shockingly. Machine gun bullets pinged off the craft's steel as they neared the shore. The boat next to him exploded into an inferno.

At the beach he dropped the gate. Water and bullets splashed in. Twenty-two of twenty-four splashed out. Leo literally kicked the butt of the last two and moved them out. Choice was not an option. They went to death and dismemberment.

The gate came up as Leo gunned the engine in reverse and watched the carnage in front of his eyes. His boat moved away and turned to get the next wave of soldiers. Alone, he let the tears fall, unashamed. They will never get off that beach he thought. Heading back to the fleet he watched as two destroyers headed towards him, towards the dangerous shallow water. As they passed him, he heard the guns open fire battering Hitler's wall.

When he arrived back at the transport he learned those two brave ships opened a hole. The survivors poured through, headed inland towards victory. He brought the next wave of soldiers to the beach, to the quiet and bloody Omaha Beach. He lowered the gate and twenty-four men simply walked off into the red tinged tide and onto the shore.

Leo had a new assignment. Help pick the dead and dismembered out of the waves.

The nightmare of that victory would follow my father for all of the fifty years he lived after D-day, until he joined the ghosts of the bodies that lay under the crosses and the stars at a beach in France, code named, Omaha.

More about Leo's life can be found in the book **Rumors about my Father.**

Excerpt from:

Rumors about my Father

Leo stood in front of Harry Klein, Deli owner and well-known Detroit bootlegger.

"Joe Rubinstein tells me you are a reliable kid who will do a good job and keep his mouth shut."

Leo didn't say anything, he just nodded.

"I have a job for you tonight," Klein said. "I want you to go with Max here. He will drive the boat, you will help with the boxes and do whatever he says. OK?"

Leo looked nervous.

"Listen kid, you don't have to worry. Max has been doing this a long time, and there is never any trouble. You don't have to carry a piece or anything. If you get busted, which you won't, just go quiet like and I'll get you out in the morning. You're a minor, it's no big deal. You understand?"

Prohibition, the noble experiment, was a nice idea, but a total failure in the 1920's and early 30's. In Detroit it was an opportunity for many people to get rich and more to get a good income. Windsor, Canada was located just across the Detroit River. Every night the river became a highway of boats bringing in the beer and whiskey for a thirsty nation.

Every boy who grew up in the Jewish neighborhood knew someone in the notorious Purple Gang, otherwise known as the Jewish mafia. As a youngster, Leo stayed away from the gangsters. Now, he was being recruited into the "Little Jewish Navy," the flotilla of high-speed boats run by the Purple Gang.

Leo was nervous as Max pulled the boat away from the pier at the end of Third Avenue, but the crossing to Canada was uneventful.

"Do you want to take the wheel?" Max asked the new recruit. "Have you ever driven a boat before?"

"No. Is it like driving a car?"

"A little, you'll get the feel, here take the controls."

Leo loved driving the boat and being out on the river. The water spraying, the speed and the assignment were all part of a new exciting adventure.

At the pier in Windsor, Leo and Max filled the boat with crates of beer and whiskey. Many bootleggers watered down the good Canadian whiskey, but Harvey Klein had a reputation of delivering the best. The on loading could be done in the open. The manifest said the booze was going to Mexico and once it left the shore, the Canadian exporters did not care where it went. In reality, they knew it was going across the river to Detroit.

The heavily loaded boat moved away from the dock and turned back to the Detroit side of the river. They proceeded in the dark without any lights. It was necessary to avoid the Coast Guard, but in fact the Little Jewish Navy's boats were better outfitted and faster. As they approached the American side, they cut the engines and quietly pulled up to the pier. A truck was waiting to take the load of alcohol to Chicago, and into the waiting storehouses of Al Capone.

As they were unloading the boxes a police patrol car pulled up.

"Holy shit!" Leo exclaimed quietly. "What do we do now?"

"Let me handle this," Max calmly replied.

Leo looked at Max. Was that a smile on his face, he wondered?

A uniformed policeman got out of the driver's side of the car and opened the trunk.

"Hi Larry," Max said, as he proceeded to place a case of beer and a case of whiskey in the trunk of the patrol car.

"Thanks Max," the officer said. "See you next time." The patrolman got back in the car and pulled away.

My dad would make this "midnight run" many times over the next year. He got to know the river and quickly learned the ropes of the Jewish Navy's import business. He was now a member of the notorious Purple Gang.

☐

Saturday Morning Heroes

When I was an eight-year-old my heroes appeared like clockwork every Saturday morning on the black and white rabbit eared way back machine. My grandfather and I would be occupied for three hours of Western justice, with lessons to be learned as important as any school, church or temple.

Grandpa Abe, a refugee of Eastern injustice, found sanctuary in the old West.

We started with the Cisco Kid, yes there was a Mexican hero on 50's TV, just no Black heroes on the black and white picture tube- but my elementary aged mind did not deal in gray moral issues yet.

Good and evil was much more black and white. The hero always won, the bad guy captured or shot without bleeding and the girl was always saved, all in a half hour show complete with Tony the Tiger commercials.

Then came the Lone Ranger with his good Indian partner Tonto; even Indians could be good guys on Saturday mornings. Long before the Beatles, my favorite tune was The William Tell Overture that ended with "High ho Silver, away."

Rin-Tin-Tin was next, starting my love affair with dogs. Before I ever had a dog, the TV German Shepard who was a member of the Western U.S. Army, saved the day and showed me the value of having a canine best friend.

We moved to the twentieth century with Roy Rogers who could drive a jeep as well as ride his horse while singing with his wife Dale Evans. He could play a guitar and a six shooter.

The morning ended with a modern day western pilot, Sky King with his lovely often imperiled niece Penny. No worries, she would get into trouble but never was she really in jeopardy. Remember on Saturday morning in the late 50's all the girls were saved, all the bad guys went to jail and all my heroes would ride off into the Western sunset.

I so enjoyed those idyllic shows of black and white while eating frosted flakes with my father's Ellis Island immigrant father.

Reality would come soon enough to take my genuine hero, my grandfather to his final sunset.

Excerpt from:

Adventures of the Omaha Kid

First Kiss

Adirondack Summer Camp

Lake George, New York

Summer 1962

Rhonda Pastrovinsky's body was changing. She was reaching puberty, developing curves, going from an awkward tomboy to a pretty young woman. The Polish-American girl, who was always teased and treated badly by the popular girls at junior high, was now attractive. Boys began to look at her differently and she liked the attention. Here at camp, all the other girls wanted to be her friend.

Carol Simon, her bunk mate, said, "I think Tim Corelli's cute. Don't you?"

"I haven't noticed." Rhonda said as she brushed her sandy brown hair. In fact, Rhonda had noticed him looking at her, and when she looked at him, he would quickly turn away. They had played this game a lot in the last few weeks, him trying to act like he wasn't looking at her.

"He won the camp tennis tournament and is so cute. I think he likes you," Carol stated.

"What makes you think so?"

"Gloria said that Roger told her that Tim told him he likes you."

Rhonda shrugged her shoulders. "Oh well, there's just two weeks of camp left. So what if he likes me."

Rhonda did like him but she had no clue how to react to this news.

The Adirondack Summer Camp was located in upstate New York near the Vermont border. It was a summer haven for mostly suburban New York and New Jersey adolescents.

The beautiful setting in the forested mountains by a large lake became the boys' and girls' natural playground. They could swim, canoe, play games and do all types of arts and crafts.

Some could even plot their first romances. Large cabins provided dorms for the kids. Girls of similar age were placed in the same cabin. Boys were grouped the same way on the other side of the mess hall.

***

The next day Rhonda decided to confront Tim. After breakfast she noticed him glancing over and walked up to him and said, "Hey Timmy, what's the deal? Why are you looking at me?"

"What do you mean?" he said, trying to be cool.

"Meet me in the trees behind the canoe dock in one hour."

"But I'm supposed to play tennis," Tim replied, as he noticed his palms sweating and his heart starting to race.

"I've heard love is supposed to mean nothing in tennis," she said with a laugh, surprising herself with her wit. She walked away and could feel her confidence growing. Tim watched her go, his mouth falling open.

***

Fourteen-year-old Tim was very comfortable on a ball field or a tennis court, but he didn't know how to deal with a pretty girl.

Especially this girl that he had spent the whole summer trying not to have her notice him sneaking glances.

He walked down the path into the forest above the canoe dock. The birch trees were in full maturity, white bark with green leaves hanging in bunches. Bees moved throughout the fertile flowers sucking the sweet nectar; summer in full bloom. He came upon the object of his obsession, Rhonda, who he noticed was wearing pink shorts, her long legs ending in white tennis shoes. Her light blue tee shirt matched her eyes. His mouth went dry.

"Hi Tim," she said with a smile on her face.

"Hi Rhonda. Why did you want me to meet you?" He heard himself saying.

"Someone said that you like me."

"I... maybe... yeah... I mean I think I might." He felt her staring right through him.

"Do you want to kiss me?"

"Sure."

Tim closed his eyes and leaned forward. Rhonda stepped forward and kissed him lightly on the lips. He could feel the hair on the back of his neck standing up. Tim would always remember that first kiss fondly.

"What are you thinking?" Rhonda asked the boy.

"I'm not sure. Maybe we should try that again."

They kissed again, trying too hard, pressing too hard. Their lips just stuck together. "How is that?" Timmy asked.

"Maybe one more time, this time softer."

Their heads moved together slowly, lips joining softly, kissing and then kissing more.

"I think we got it right that time," the nervous girl said giggling.

In the next two weeks, they would sneak off and kiss. It was puppy love. Timmy felt so wonderful, so horrible and so unsatisfied.

When camp ended, their parents showed up to take them home. They could not even kiss goodbye. As they drove south in separate cars, going their separate ways, Rhonda cried and Tim smiled.

Praise for:

The Adventures of the Omaha Kid
Colin Alkars, writer, poet

I was initially attracted to this book for its sports themes, but this novel is much more than the story of a remarkable athlete.

"The Adventures of the Omaha Kid" engagingly explores themes of identity and relationship - how we go about defining ourselves and finding our place in the world. Winters is a gifted storyteller. His narrative is inventive and his characters are drawn with confidence and care. You'll enjoy your encounter with "The Omaha Kid."

Bob has created something really special…with complex characters…I couldn't put it down. Dorothy Mackay Collins Former curator, Robert Lewis Stevenson Museum

Bob has a great story telling ability. Ken Klein, author of Thailand Stories

Excerpt from:

Finding Shelter from the Cold

A fictional look at the story of how wolves started on the evolution to become dogs, based on the latest and best scientific evidence.

What is being said about Finding Shelter:

The writing reminds me of Jack London a great adventure for teens and dog lovers of all ages Jenny Pessereau, Author

"I love this book." Barbara Nemko, Napa Superintendent of Schools

Prologue

The wolf glided quickly across the field wearing a thick coat of winter white fur. She had picked out her prey, a large deer with huge antlers.

The buck was in rut and had just lost a battle to another male, fighting for sexual dominance. He was gasping for breath.

It was cold, Ice Age cold. Icicles clung to the trees. Frozen tundra met the forest where the river ice was like glass.

The elk's head bobbed up and down as his antlers scraped against the white fir's tree bark. Foam dripped from the buck's mouth and steam rose from his nostrils. He was powerful but exhausted in defeat, vulnerable.

The lone wolf growled and started the attack, chasing the large mammal. Even in his fatigue, the elk was quick. He bounded off, outpacing the sprinting wolf.

The prey ran for open space, away from the trees, putting fifty yards between himself and his attacker. The buck slowed, catching his breath, when the next wolf jumped out.

The male leader of the pack had been hiding in plain sight, white on white, lying flat on the ice. He sprung, powerful legs projecting him towards his prey.

The rest of the pack chased the buck in tandem, till the exhausted elk turned to face his foes.

There were five in the pack; a snowy white male with a black spot on his muzzle and four females, including the alpha-bitch with a brown spot on her tail. All the wolves were camouflaged blending with their icy surroundings.

The full pack surrounded the vanquished buck. Still formidable, but out of breath, he lowered his antlers ready to charge. The wolves took turns snapping at his hind legs, away from his dangerous rack. Helpless, the poor creature turned in circles trying to fend them off, his very life at stake. The five canines bore into him, tearing the elk's flesh with powerful jaws and sharp teeth. Blood flowed, turning white coats red. They ripped into chunks of meat which they quickly devoured.

As twilight descended, sending a glow into the western sky, the frosty air got even colder. Suddenly, a loud roar perked up their ears, distracting them from their meal.

The pack looked up to see two huge white arctic lions approaching. The big cats had smelled blood and wanted to poach the kill. As deadly as a pack of wolves could be, they were no match for the oversized lions.

The male wolf, reluctant to yield, growled, teeth flashing. He tried to defend the carcass.

The great white male lion with the frosty mane swiped with deadly claws, catching the hesitant wolf along his right side, leaving a huge gash. The wolf's blood flowed, mixed with the elk's alredy on his coat. He finally retreated, mortally wounded. The sky darkened, night descended quickly. The young male wolf lay dying.

Chapter 1

The Wolf's Story

I hold my tail high because I'm the alpha-bitch, proud. I have earned my position by guile, guts and glory. The other females do not have what it takes to be leader. I plan, I sniff out shelter and lead the pack, while the male lies about, recharging for his next sexual escapade. He is the figurative absolute leader, but I do most of the real work.

With Blackthroat down and dying, the pack looks to me to take charge; to lead. How stupid he was to challenge a lion. Though males tend to be that way; not knowing when to retreat, when to give up the fight. He lay on the ice whimpering, my lover, my friend, our leader.

Without another male in the pack, six eyes looked at me to lead them. What to do? I nuzzled my fallen mate. He groaned. I licked his face and turned away. With a nod to the rest of the pack, we left. A wounded wolf brings all types of predators.

Temperatures were falling. I could smell snow in the air, and we needed shelter from the storm. We headed to a small cave that we had dug under a rock in the cool mud last summer.

It was not too far away and it was time to go. We jogged to the cave, our bellies half full but our hearts empty. We crawled under our rock and lay tightly together to share our body heat against the wicked night's cold. Exhausted, we fell into a restless sleep, knowing our pack must change. Our pack needed a male.

The morning dawned colder and wetter. Snow had fallen during the night and crunched under my paws. I liked to walk alone at times, to get away from the others and think.

As clouds hung in the sky, I walked to the ridgetop to watch the two-legged wolves. They didn't have fur but wore skin from animals on their backs. They lived in huts during the summer by the icy river. I could see tree branches and stretched hide that made their shelters.

I called them two-legged wolves because they were smart like us. Like wolves, they hunt in packs, taking turns chasing their prey or laying in ambush like we would. But on their front paws they had these long digits. They held tools to hunt; long sticks with points or weighted sticks with stones.

They needed these tools because they couldn't run fast and their teeth were pathetic.

Gray Ears, my sister, followed my scent to the ridge. She was the smallest of the pack so her tail was always down between her hind legs. She came to me and rolled on her back offering her belly in submission. I licked her on the mouth in greeting.

Gray Ears rose up with a look on her face that asked "What are you doing?"

I nodded toward the human huts. She shrugged her shoulders. She didn't understand my fascination with them. Somehow, I knew humans and wolves were linked.

Still Finding Shelter from the Cold

White wolf glides quietly, stalking her prey

prehistoric icy wonderland

buck locked in her sight

she springs, diving across the tundra

reindeer flees, eyes escape, evergreens ahead

the pack waits

white on white invisible silent

six pack-mates strike

powerful jaws take hold,

tight knife-like grip

teeth rip,

red flows on white

seven canines consume chunks of meat

leaving little for scavengers

pack prances away, bellies full

someday their distant descendants

will spring, diving into the SUV

going home with you and me.

Past the Future started out as a Halloween short story until I remade it into a novel.

Here it is in its original form:

2125 AD

I'm so groggy but try to focus. Where am I? How did I get here? A strange elevator music played in my head, without earphones, or any noticeable speaker. I hear an advertisement, with a totally absurd and scary notion. It grabs my attention and shakes me awake:

Sony-Audi-Google--SAG--is proud to unveil the latest in baby technology for 2125. As everyone knows, you must start a new baby with a great mother-board. Our new model comes with our highly improved mother-board with 1,000,000 gigs of RAM and the latest in stem cell developments. SAG's new "Jordish" model comes with an asexual uni-body, patent pending, guaranteed to last 200 years or 1,000,000 miles, whichever comes first. All races' genetic codes are included, and the new model adds five new skin shades for a total choice of 50 glorious colors.

The new mother-board put last year's brain-core to shame, with twice the memory and three times the speed. No need for that old embarrassing, messy sex. Sexual problems are distant memories as our uni-body is totally sex free.

Your new baby now comes from the most sterile assembly line, fed the best liquid nutrition. No breast milk needed. So, when you are ready to complete your family, think of Sony-Audi-Google. Remember: When you are ready, SAG is ready for you.

Yes, I am awake now. What in the hell was that? It's the first thing I hear as I come out of my induced coma. It appears I am a twenty-first century man waking up in the twenty-second century.

***

2052 AD

The United States, which by 2052 included Canada and Mexico, returned to manned space flight after The United Arab States started their space program. There's nothing like a new cold war to induce space innovation. The Arabs and all their oil money decided to explore space and wanted to land on one of Saturn's or Jupiter's moons to look for natural resources. Most commodities on earth were getting scarce.

The last thing I can remember -- before my mind picked up this baby advertisement -- I was rocketing on an experimental flight to Titan, Saturn's biggest moon.

My robot companion, Mercury, named after the first group of US manned spaceships, warned: "Dave, something is seriously wrong with the spaceship. Fuel has been leaking. I am going to implement emergency alternative 'Van-Winkle.'"

"Are you sure, Mercury? That's a pretty radical program," I said.

It would mean all other options for safe return to Earth were not available. It would put me into an induced coma, inside a life- support bubble. The ship's other programs would be shut down and I would drift in space until NASA Control could find some way to rescue me. This alternative was experimental. While the Van-Winkle program had been coded into this type of spacecraft, it had never been used. It was the last resort for a desperate situation.

"Yes, Dave, that is the only way to save you. I am sorry. Good luck Dave. You will be asleep in 10, 9, 8, 7, 6, 5, 4, 3, 2...."

2125AD

Consciousness comes in this new century. That ad slapped me awake. Hospital buzzers sounded and a team of workers come running to my aid.

"Welcome to 2125," the strange looking man said with what I think is a smile, "I am Jordish-Michael 7062, your lead doctor. You are a lucky man. Virgin-Boeing Space found your spacecraft drifting outside the solar system. They pulled your craft back to earth."

"An examination shows that your central nervous system was still alive. Our stem cell technology replaced all your damaged body systems."

The new-style man talking to me had a humongous head. His skin was bright green. Each of his hands had seven fingers: four fingers and three opposing thumbs.

"Thank you," is all I could manage to say, totally unnerved and shocked, as I realized I had been drifting in space for 73 years.

***

My skeletal system has been replaced and must harden. Organs have been repaired or replaced. I'm told I will have the body of a healthy 25-year-old man when everything heals.

Trapped in the hospital, Modern novels and teleported shows are beamed straight into my head in 3D, teaching me about society in the 22nd century. War and disease are a thing of the past. The new models of humanity have been genetically programed to cooperate. They appear amazingly intelligent. Genetic engineering has defeated mental illness.

With all these advancements, I feel something is missing. The architecture, dance and music of this culture are beautiful but boringly similar. Everything looks and sounds the same, lacking what 20th century rockers called soul. It sounds like elevator music.

After more 22nd century novels are beamed to my brain, I realize what is missing. Without the crazy genotype, they have lost the rebels, the true creators. These modern "humans" are genetically programed to get along, go with the flow. Innovation is sacrificed.

Radical change in style is stifled. There are no Kurt Vonnegut's, Thomas Jefferson's, H.G.Wells or Susan B. Anthony's in this environment. Without mutation and natural selection, humanity seems stuck on a treadmill going nowhere.

Unfortunately, I have more immediate and personal worries. I have to get out of this God-forsaken hospital. But I'm trapped. My new bones are not yet hardened enough for me to walk. Jordish-Michael 7062 is planning to do surgery on me tomorrow, modernizing me.

I'm getting an antenna implanted, and 7062 also scheduled surgery to remove my "unnecessary" sex organ.

Still in a Halloween mood; try this short story:

Friday the Fourteenth

It was not a great day for Wendy Paterson. The nineteen-year old girl had not done well on her economics test at Merritt College. Wendy met with the instructor, Mr. Tanner and the creep made a pass at her. She showed her contempt and told him off, and now she was worried about her grade. She was used to guys her age flirting with her, but not her teacher. It had made her very uncomfortable.

Wendy had long blond hair, striking blue eyes, and the slim figure of a runner; she was on the track team. Her long legs helped her stride in the distance races. As she left the classroom building, she looked out at the pouring rain coming down in the Oakland hills, on this ominous January day at four in the afternoon, darkness rushed towards her.

Damn, she thought to herself. This day just keeps getting worse. She pulled up the hood on her jacket and made a beeline to the parking lot, jogging as her book bag bounced on her back.

She was wearing high-heeled shoes and they were not easy to run with on the wet sidewalk. She slipped, broke a heel, and fell headlong into a wet bush, skinning her knee.

Wendy was wet and limping as she approached her car. She found her keys, opened the door and disgusted, threw her books across to the passenger seat. As the starter cranked over, the car would not kick alive. "Come on, come on, please start," she said out loud to her five-year-old Honda that her parents had bought her to commute to college. On the third try the engine finally turned over, coming to life. The inside of the windshield was covered with moisture and she blasted the defroster and started the windshield wipers.

Putting the car into gear, Wendy fought to see out the windshield as the rain and fog devoured the automobile.

Carefully she turned out of the parking lot and headed for home. Wendy was still living at home in the suburbs of the Oakland Hills. The house of her childhood was a three-bedroom located on a cul-de-sac about ten miles north of the college campus.

Her radio was tuned to KCBS, the San Francisco news station. A woman had been attacked near her neighborhood two days earlier and she wanted to hear if there were any details on the radio.

There was the sports report and the weather, then some national news. When the local report came on she started paying close attention.

"Sam Harvey is reporting from the Oakland Police Department with the latest news on the attack of a woman Wednesday in the upper Piedmont area. Sam..."

"Joel, the police are reporting that the woman was brutally attacked and sexually assaulted. She is in critical condition at Highland Hospital. The name of the women is being withheld. There are no suspects in this heinous crime at this time. The police are asking for anyone with any information to call their hotline at 551-Tips. A-five-hundred-dollar reward has been offered for any information leading to the arrest of the person who committed this crime. This is Sam Harvey reporting from the Oakland Police department."

"Thanks Sam, what was that number again?"

"Joel, that's 551-Tips."

Wendy's cell phone rang.

"Hello," she said, her hands-free device turned down the radio.

"Wendy, it's Mom, did you hear about the assault? Where are you?"

"Yah, I was just listening to the radio. It's awful close to home. Kinda scary, I'll be careful though. I just left school and I'm on the way home."

"How was your day?"

"Terrible, Wendy sighed, I'll tell you about it when I get home."

"Ok, bye hon, drive safe."

"Bye Mom, see you soon."

It started raining harder and the wind was blowing the wet eucalyptus leaves across the blacktop. The Honda went around a curve and the back tires skidded across the street. Wendy steered into the skid, remembering her driver's education classes from high school. The car straightened, but she stopped the car by the side of the road a minute to catch her breath and to let her heart slow down. As Wendy's foot came off the brake, she stepped on the gas, the car stalled.

"Damn!" She yelled.

She moved the shifter back into park and turned the key. Nothing happened, the battery was dead. Wendy took out her cell phone and hit speed dial to her Mom, no signal! She could not believe her bad luck. Let's see, she thought, it was Friday, but the thirteenth was yesterday. What to do? It was still raining "cats and dogs," and she was still a half-mile from her house. She thought about her broken shoe. Screw it, she thought, I'll leave my stuff in the car and walk home barefoot. She zipped up her jacket, pulled up her hood and started walking home.

Darkness was almost complete, the rain and fog grabbed at her jacket. She had to lean into the wind. Before she walked two blocks, she was wet, cold, and shivering in the evening's embrace. Wendy turned the corner into her housing complex and walked past Hillside Elementary School, where years earlier she had been a student. Soaked through to her bones, she was only four blocks from home.

Out of the corner of her eye she thought she saw a shadow behind a tree by the elementary school. Was that a person? She quickened her pace and thought she heard someone behind her. She looked back quickly and only saw fog, and rain coming down. This is my imagination playing a trick on me, she thought. I'm cold, wet and tired and just need to get home. Get it together, you have made this trip from school thousands of times.

Am I paranoid, is something real to fear? She wondered. That crazy rapist is still out there somewhere. Could he be behind her? She looked back again; was that a shadow behind her in the fog? No, she didn't think so. It was strange, her neighborhood usually was quiet, but now there were no cars at all. She was just two blocks from her house. I'm ok, she thought.

Yes, she heard someone behind her. As she looked back, she saw a man duck behind a tree. Wendy started to run. She could now hear footsteps. The person behind her was running! Wendy was a block from her house and had to turn a corner.

She slipped on her wet nylon encased feet and fell. Her knee slammed into the sidewalk. Blood from her knee mixed with the water from the rain and ran down her leg. Wendy was back up in an instant and running again.

She didn't look back but could hear the footsteps getting closer. She was at her house! But he was right behind her. Turning toward the shadowy figure, she screamed at the top of her lungs.

Her fifteen-year old younger brother, Phillip, was staring her in the face.

"Wow, Wendy that was quite a scream. Did I scare you? Sorry," he said sarcastically, a smile on his face.

Wendy looked at him and did not know to hit him or hug him. "You are going to be so sorry!" she said.

Then to Phillip's dismay. Wendy hugged her brother and cried on his shoulder.

My Memoir is called **Not Quite Kosher**. This excerpt is an example of why that title fits:

High Holy Daze Day Dream

God turned to his heavenly counsel of Gandhi, Buddha, Jesus, Mohammad and Moses, a look of disgust occupied his bearded face.

"Those religious fanatics are playing God again," he thundered.

"Which ones this time?" Gandhi asked.

"All of them: Moslems, Christians, Hindus and Jews; each think they are the only path to righteousness; claim to know what I want. Then they have to fight each other in wars to satisfy their delusions. Jesus, why didn't they get your message of peace when I sent you there?"

"Lord did you forget that whole Crucifixion thing?"

"Of course not, I just was hoping that they might evolve faster. I worked almost all of day four on that evolution plan." He shook his head in sadness.

"I spent a good deal of time making women as attractive as the flowers in bloom. Yet all the extreme religious zealots want to do is tell those amazing beauties to cover up their bodies. That amount of loveliness is one of my greatest works.

And don't get me started about the nature thing again; it took me almost a whole day of creation, to balance the whole climate thing. Those big brained monkeys screw up my perfect atmosphere in just one century, cutting down trees and producing greenhouse gases. When the resulting climate change causes floods, famine and hurricanes; they have the nerve to call it an act of God. Sometimes I feel like that Jewish comedian."

"Woody Allen?" Gandhi asked.

"No, Rodney Dangerfield. "I get no respect.'"

Moses suggested. "Maybe it's time you want to come down with your wrath."

"No." God sighed. "I've tried that. They never learn."

"So, what are you going to do?" Mohammad asked.

"I think I'll just let them deal with their own Karma."

Another High Holy Daze Dream

(I wrote this before the Russian Olympics or the Cubs winning the World Series)

God's heavenly counsel of Moses, Jesus, Gandhi, Buddha, Mohamed were hearing the big guy rant again

"Can't those earthlings get anything right?"

'Mohamed, I said swords into plowshares not make IUD's"

"That's IEDs Lord," Mohamed reminded him, my followers say a lot of things I didn't say."

"Yeah, God said, "I can relate"

"Who can keep track of all the stuff they make to kill each other. Maybe it's time to send another message; I mean Paris, so beautiful." He shook his head.

"It's been a while since I sent words to that guy in upstate NY; I like what they did in Utah, but when I told him to multiply I was being literal, their SAT math scores could use improvement. I did not mean take more wives."

Moses said, "Let's do the Five-Commandment thing again, that worked we... maybe not."

"OK" God said, "Let's wait another year, I heard the Cubs might be good, and I'd like to see that; then, the Olympics in Moscow, I love the ballet. Besides if we just wait a few more years they will be mostly under water."

"Many Christians don't believe that," Gandhi said.

"Neither did Noah." God reminded them.

The late great General and President Dwight Eisenhower told us to "Beware of the Military Industrial Complex." Maybe we should have paid closer attention.

While I believe the fighting of wars are almost always a mistake, I have written many stories about battle. Here are a few:

The Round Trip

Joe Buckman kissed Lisa and held her in a long embrace. He felt her body next to his and he did not want to let go; like he was taking a mental picture of the feeling. He didn't know when or if he would ever kiss her again.

They had met two weeks earlier in San Francisco, at a Grateful Dead Concert. He had two weeks leave after completing school to be a Personnelman in the Navy. He was 19, the average age of the young men who were dying in Vietnam. She was 18, a senior at Berkeley High School. Since they met at the beginning of August, they had been together every day.

She had long blond hair, wore love beads and bellbottom pants; the uniform of the anti-war movement in

1970. He also wore bellbottoms, the uniform of the United States Navy.

Lisa gave him a ride to Travis Air force Base to catch a plane. His orders told him to report to the USS Gulf Stream, ARS 53, a rescue salvage ship, which was presently located in Da Nang Harbor, Vietnam.

They listened to rock and roll on the radio in her Volkswagen Bug, when the music was interrupted by a speech from President Richard Nixon.

"Let me make one thing perfectly clear, the war in Vietnam is winding down. I have a secret plan to end the war."

"If that's true, what the hell am I going for?" Petty Officer Buckman asked.

"I could keep driving and take you to Canada."

"No, this is something I've got to do."

He felt very confused. He had been in the Navy for just over a year, enlisting just out of high school. At first, he was proud to wear the uniform, but the more he thought about the war in Vietnam, the more he realized he didn't want to go.

As Mohammad Ali said, "I've got nothing against these Vietnamese."

At the front gate of the Air Force Base. He kissed her again.

"I can't wait to see you when I come back."

"I'd like that, sailor man."

He let her go, turned and walked to the guardhouse at the front gate. He looked back at her. She held up two fingers. "Peace," she yelled at him. He saluted the guard, showed his orders and was directed to the chartered aircraft sitting on the runway. The next stop would be Clark Air Force Base in the Philippines, then on to Da Nang.

***

Joe Buckman descended the stairs of the Air Force transport. The heat and humidity hit him like an Ali left hook. Within minutes sweat was coming through his dress white uniform. He walked into the terminal and showed the information officer his orders. He was told to have a seat and someone would be with him shortly. Oh yes, he thought, the old military hurry up and wait. He took a seat, and in spite of the fact that it was ten in the morning, lack of sleep and major jet lag allowed him to fall asleep in the chair.

"Are you Buckman?"

Joe looked up to see a black Navy petty officer staring down at him.

"Ah, yeah," he said groggily, trying to focus his eyes. "How long..."

He looked at his watch. "It's 1300 hours."

"I'm Perry. I've come to take you to the ship."

"Ok, thanks, let me get my sea bag."

"I've got a jeep out front," Perry said.

They moved out of the terminal and Perry loaded the sea bag into the back of the jeep.

"I am very glad to see you," Perry said. "You are my ticket out. Personnelman Buckman, the Gulf Stream is all yours, I'm going home tomorrow. You're my replacement. I'll show you some of your duties here.

"You need to get the ship's mail at the Navy base."

"What's the ship like?" Buckman asked.

"It's an old rust bucket, built for World War II. It's slow and small. One 40mm gun is the only defense, and if you have to use it, you are in real trouble.

Half of the eighty-man crew are divers, doing rescue and salvage work. The captain is an old enlisted man who worked himself up to Lieutenant Commander the hard way; does everything by the book. The Ex-O is your boss. He's a hard-ass Lieutenant, just a year out of Annapolis. And Ortiz, the first-class gunner's mate, is a first-class jerk, watch out for him. Hey, do you get high?"

"Yeah, of course, I was at a Dead concert last week. Everyone I know who's our age smokes weed."

Perry produced a joint and smiled. "The guys on the ship will want you to get some when you get the mail. You can buy it in what appears to look like cigarette cartons, tax stamped and everything."

"Aren't you worried about getting caught?" Buckman asked.

"No, I'm not, I know where to go and I'm careful."

The two drove down an alley and took a smoke break. Then they went back to the Navy base and did the mail run. Finally, they drove the jeep back to the ship.

Buckman looked at the Gulf Stream. He was assigned to this ship for the next year. It was small; an oversize tugboat. He boarded the ship, carrying his sea bag over his shoulder. He saluted the duty petty officer.

"Permission to come aboard, sir," he said, showing his orders.

"Permission granted."

And just like that, Buckman was a member of the crew.

Perry took Buckman to see the Executive Officer, Lt. Schulman; then down to his quarters to stow his gear. He was given one small locker and a bunk second from the top. The bunks were stretched canvas, stacked four high. Next to the four "racks," as they were called, was a post and then four more racks. Quarters were very cramped. What could not fit in your two-foot by two-foot locker, was kept in your sea bag, to be placed in the forward hold.

Perry took Buckman to the small office, consisting of two desks, one for yeoman, Tim Larson, and one for him. A Royal manual typewriter was locked down to the desk. Everything had to be locked down, for times of rough seas. Buckman noticed that he was not seasick but was feeling woozy and the ship was still tied to the peer. It was his first sea duty. He wondered how he would feel when the ship got underway.

The next day, Buckman said goodbye to Perry.

"Good luck," Buckman said.

"You're the one who needs luck, man, I'm going home," Perry replied, and laughed.

Joe watched as Perry saluted the duty officer, the flag on the fantail, and walked off the ship. It was Joe's job now, ready or not.

"All hands to special sea detail stations," the order came from the bridge. Buckman made his way to the control center. He would only watch today, learning his job; a captain's phone talker during sea detail and general quarter's station.

The ship was headed to the DMZ near the border with North Vietnam. An oil tanker had hit a mine and put itself aground to avoid sinking. It was the Gulf Stream's job to use its divers to patch the ship and tow it back to sea. At all ahead standard, the ship made ten knots. It would take all day to get to station.

The sun was setting when the grounded tanker came into view. Buckman looked at the wounded ship on the beach. Oil was leaking into the water and onto a beautiful, clear, coral reef. The jungle came right down to the beach. He thought that this would be the perfect vacation spot if it weren't for this nasty little war. The Gulf Stream dropped anchor and posted guard fore and aft. They would wait until morning to start the arduous task of getting the tanker seaworthy.

In the morning the Gulf Stream moved in close to shore. The workboat was launched, filled with divers to begin patching the hole in the oil tanker. Not being a diver, Buckman was given the job of securing a perimeter around the tanker. Ten men from the Gulf Stream were given old M-1 rifles and joined ten members of the tanker crew on guard duty ashore around the workstation. Six divers put on their gear and started working on the patch.

Without warning all hell broke loose. Mortar shells rained down from the sky. The sailors on the beach opened fire with their rifles but were firing blindly into the jungle. A shell hit the tanker and a fire broke out. From the Gulf Stream's bridge, a call for help went out to the fleet. Fifty miles away, two A-4 Phantoms took off from an aircraft carrier and headed to the rescue like John Wayne and the cavalry in a Western Movie. But Vietnam was not Hollywood. A mortar fell close to Buckman. Both his legs felt like they were on fire. He looked down and blood was covering his legs.

"Help, someone help!" he yelled.

The ship's corpsmen ran to his side, putting a tourniquet on each leg. Just then they could hear the jets, as the jungle exploded in napalm fire from bombs dropped by the Navy aircraft.

Other sailors appeared with a stretcher and they removed the wounded petty officer from the beach and placed him in the workboat. He passed out.

***

Buckman awoke with his head in a fog. He was in a helicopter, a morphine drip in his arm. He could not even feel his legs. Were they ok? He didn't know. He stayed in a fog for days, not sure where he was or where he was going. Did he awake on an aircraft? He wasn't sure.

It was a full ten days later that he awoke with consciousness. He was in a hospital. His eyes began to focus. Seeing a morphine drip next to his bed attached to his arm, he felt for his legs. They were gone.

Tears streamed from his eyes and depression hit him hard. He learned he was at the naval hospital in Oakland, California. The doctors told him he would be fitted with artificial limbs.

He thought about Lisa, so close, over in Berkeley. He didn't want her to see him like this and couldn't bring himself to call her. His parents came to see him all the way from Pennsylvania. They were happy to see their son, glad he was alive, but he could see the sadness in their faces. They stayed for a week and then headed home. When they left, he felt empty, alone.

In December, Joe Buckman left the hospital for the first time, alone. He was in a wheelchair. He took a taxi into San Francisco and told the cabby to drive him around town. He had three months back pay in his pocket; he could afford the cab fare. Over Nob Hill the taxi went, as he watched the tourists board the cable car; something he could not do. Then it was past Chinatown to North Beach.

"Take me to Sausalito," he said.

The cab turned, heading for the Golden Gate Bridge. Joe thought of Lisa and how he would never see her again.

As they got to the bridge, Buckman said to the cab driver, "I've changed my mind. Let me out here."

"Are you sure; here?"

"Yah, help me get the wheelchair out." After he was safely in the chair, he gave the driver a hundred-dollar bill.

"Thanks, keep the change."

He wheeled the chair onto the bridge with the walkers and bike riders and set out across the landmark. The cold wind slapped his face and fog fought against the last bit of sunshine over the Pacific.

A purple and red glow appeared on the horizon. Waves crashed below the bridge. Even in the cold air,

Buckman broke into a sweat from the work of moving his wheelchair along the walkway.

As he neared the middle of the bridge, he stopped and looked longingly back at the city he loved. He looked down at the cold ocean water that never saw sunlight in the bridge's shadow. The waves foamed like saliva in a wolf's mouth just before his carnal bite.

Joe pulled himself out of his chair and dropped over the railing.

How long did he fall? One second? Two? Did he see his whole life flash before his eyes? No; just the part where he was in his mother's arms. Or was it the arms of his lover in Berkeley? For just that second, he felt warmth.

Joe Buckman's name does not appear on the Vietnam Memorial. His death was a suicide. But surely his life ended in Vietnam, like the innocence of a generation.

That story was fiction.

The next story about Vietnam is factual. Rick Hegner employed me to write his biography:

Excerpt from:

The Rick Hegner Story.

Living on the Edge

Bong Son, Vietnam

When Rick arrived in Vietnam, his sweat glands started working overtime. He'd never felt that combination of heat and humidity before and he continued to swelter throughout his deployment. From the first time he heard distant gun fire, his mind went on alert, edging on paranoia, feeling a hostile vibe and recognizing that nowhere was safe. "Watch your back," became a type of greeting.

Captain Hegner's job was to run the interrogation unit, which he realized was filled with a first-rate group of men. Unfortunately, the CO, his direct boss and tent mate was a total doofus, a lot like the fictional idiot, Major Burns in the TV show, Mash.

Rick attacked his job with the vigor he had shown in learning Russian. His unit interrogated NVA and VC captives; tasked to get useful information from the prisoners, like troop movements. They had translators assigned to his command to help in the interrogations. It turned out to be more frustrating than fruitful because by the time the POW's arrived to his unit; the information they were able to get was too tardy to be useful. Every once in a while, he got lucky and some tidbit turned out to be significant.

Occasionally, Rick was called out into the field to work, which meant flying in a chopper to a battlefield. The chopper was flying low over a forward position, when "BANG," a round came right through the nose of the helicopter leaving a gaping hole right in front of him. The thud of impact sent a rush of adrenaline blasting through his body. The pilot made a quick evasive maneuver that scared the hell out of him almost as much as the impact of the shell. When they landed, the pilot told him, "We were just lucky it was a dud; if it had exploded we would have been toast."

"That shit was scary as hell!" Rick replied, still shaking.

***

Rick played a trick on a wounded NVA soldier to get information during an ongoing battle. He gave the man two aspirin, telling him they were pain pills. After the enemy soldier washed them down, Rick told him, "The pills were really poison, I have the antidote and I will give it to you if you tell me what I want to know."

The NVA soldier just shook his head. Rick's conscience bothered him. He gave the phony antidote to a nurse to give to the man after he left. He realized he was no good at playing dirty pool.

***

At base camp Rick did his best to drop a few lines to Priscilla each night. Her letters meant so much to him and the care packages with all types of goodies were heaven sent. They sent audio tapes back and forth, but the sound of her voice just made him miss her even more.

She wrote him about her drafting job, for unmanned space probes, at the Jet Propulsion Lab in Pasadena. She told him how much fun it was living with her parents as equal adults and about Joe. The dog was such a comfort to her with Rick being away. One day, she was paged at work to come home. Her father told her, Joe was barking at the front door when he just collapsed and died. They wrapped the dog in a blanket and buried him in the backyard. Rick felt her tears and wished he could hold her in his arms.

***

Priscilla watched with horror as the news about the war played out on television each night. Especially disconcerting was the

Tet Offensive, when the NVA and Viet Cong launched a large-scale attack that put the U.S. on the defensive for a while.

Vietnam was the first war that was broadcast live on television. For those like Priscilla, with loved ones fighting, it was very hard to watch.

Rick wrote her that he heard the fighting nearby but his unit escaped harm.

***

Camp Evans

After three months on the front lines at Bong Son, Rick's unit moved out by jeep convoy. They were wearing flak-jackets to protect them from flying bullets and shrapnel. On the coast, they boarded a small flat bottomed LFT, a landing craft. The boat sailed south and rocked and rolled more than Elvis' hips, as it moved down the coast at night to the Marine Base at Da Nang. Seasick, Rick was happy to get off the darn thing.

After finding their billet for the night, Lt. Foster and Rick went exploring. Da Nang was a major port with a large Marine facility, protecting the harbor and Air Force Base.

Rick was pleasantly surprised when they reached Army Camp Evans because it had actual structures.

An officer's mess, enlisted mess and decent latrines awaited them. It was still a tent city but one step up at the time, he thought.

Rick was Executive Officer; second in command, standing outside the Order of Battle tent, when he heard the distinct whine of an incoming mortar round. He dove for the ground and crawled to the bunker as the first one exploded. Twenty mortars and seventeen rockets fell around the camp, causing destruction.

After a quiet pause, Rick arose and returned to his tent. A round had gone through his sleeping bag, flattened his air mattress and was sticking out of his desk and file cabinet. Three of his men were critically wounded, taken to triage but could not be saved.

Rick had the unenviable task of writing letters to their families; one of the most difficult things he ever had to do.

***

A full month after the attack, the major networks reported that Camp Evans was totally destroyed. Rick would have laughed off the mistake, except for the heartache he knew that report would cause back home. He never really trusted the media again.

***

Priscilla went about her normal business, trying to occupy her time. She thought, "No news was good news." When no one and no letter came to her door in the normal 48-hour notification time period, she felt slightly better.

Finally, she received Rick's letter explaining the attack and she felt she could breathe again.

After a year in the field, Rick's orders arrived to depart the front lines and head home to the States. Typical of the Army, he never received orders about the methodology to accomplish this task. He decided not to tempt fate and to find his own way to get out of danger and find a way home. He made some miraculous connections and finally found himself taking off on a transport jet to Travis Air Force Base. It rolled down the runway and when it lifted into the sky the departing personal gave a loud cheer.

Not having a chance before he left, Rick called Pricilla the second he landed. She screamed with joy and surprise upon hearing his voice and jumped into the car. Soon they were in each other's arms.

A DOUBLE AGENT

Veteran's day now over and gone.

I must admit I get a little nervous,

when people thank me for my service.

It's hard to get beyond my part in Vietnam.

I have to say I feel some guilt

about serving in a war that was built

on so many president's and general's lies.

Can anybody give me the reason whys?

Thought I was done with that war when I left the ship.

Appears body and conscience won't let it slip,

as Agent Orange would later awake,

some forty years later and cause me to shake.

The next short story is the first prose piece I wrote back in

1973 for a class on, writing historical fiction at Sonoma State.

Of course, it has been rewritten and edited since then.

By the way I earned an A.

The Other Band of Brothers

October, 1415

The river galloped downstream, fed all day by the heavy rain. Wind whipped its way through the Bay road enduing many a nasty winter. The old oak's naked branches reached up like it was trying to surrender to the storm. Under those branches a man rode by on a black horse. Steam rose from the tired horse's nostrils as it tried to breathe in the thick, humid, air. The tired animal struggled to take another step.

The man slumped in the saddle with his eyes closed. Sleep tried to overtake him. A coat of steel covered his body like an insect with an exoskeleton. A long lance was lashed to the side of his muddy leather war saddle. A steel shield hung opposite, counterbalancing the lance. Two arrows stuck out from the silver fox painted on the shield.

If I don't find shelter soon, he thought, I shall fall to the muddy earth and meet my savior, who through his mercy has spared me in battle. Long brown hair came down to his shoulders, sliding down below his metal helmet. The armed man tried to shake his groggy brown eyes open but fatigue would not allow him to see more than a blur. Yet on he pushed, hoping against hope to find shelter soon.

Night attacked the daylight in the diurnal battle that the darkness always won. The sky showed a darker shade of grey in the transition. Clouds blocked the rising moon and stars. The man almost fell from his mount. Catching himself, he opened his bloodshot eyes to see a light in the distance. Focusing, he made out a building a mile or so in the direction he was riding.

"Yes!" He cried out loud and spurred his mount to a trot, arriving at his destination minutes later. As the young knight dismounted, he noticed the light go out between the cracks of the door. The building had the markings of an inn made of wood and standing shabbily, in need of repair. A small stable stood in the back.

He knocked on the door, only to be answered by silence. Again, he rapped on the door, without hearing an answer.

"Is anyone there?" he yelled, still no answer.

"Open or I shall break the door down!" he shouted angrily.

"Please go away," a women's voice begged from behind the closed door.

Surprised by the reply, the soldier mellowed, "Please, I am cold, tired, and hungry. Surely a good Christian cannot refuse me."

"But you are dressed for war," the woman replied, fear in her voice. The door remained closed.

"I mean no harm, and I can pay for my keep," the knight assured her.

The door opened slowly and a young woman stood in front of the solider. His heart almost stopped and his mouth dropped open at the sight of her. He thought he must have fallen in the mud and this was the gates of heaven, for in front of him stood an angel.

Her long golden hair fell down to her slim waist. She wore a simple dress tied in the middle and her bare feet looked cold and pale. Her blue eyes showed fright, turning away from his gaze. The man stood speechless.

"Well come in," she said softly, "or we will all die from the cold."

A fire blazed in its place by the side wall. A young boy sat by it. He too had golden hair, and blue eyes. The knight assumed he was the young woman's brother.

"I would like very much to be out of my armor," the knight begged.

The boy and maiden succeeded in helping the young man out of his armor.

The woman offered him a meal of acorn bread and warm cider. He tore into the meal without talking. She watched him, also in silence.

When he finished, he said, "I would like a room for the night."

"The inn has been closed for months, none of the rooms are made up or fit to sleep in. The storm is very bad, so you may stay here by the fire until it ends," the young woman said.

"But where is the inn keeper?" asked the knight, looking about the room.

"The plague has taken both of my parents," the girl replied. Her voice cracked and she became silent.

"I see," said the solider. Minutes later, exhausted, he fell asleep on the lambskin rug near the fireplace.

The young woman stooped to cover him but stopped long enough to look at his broad shoulders and strong hands. After he was covered, she gazed into his attractive young bearded face.

What makes men go to war, she thought, and turned to her brother. He looked with awe at the metal armor, drying on the other side of the room.

"When I grow up, I will be a great knight and save a king in battle," he said, but knew a poor boy like him had little chance to purchase a soldier's weapons.

The woman stood up and pointed to the door. "Go put the soldier's horse in the stable."

He obeyed at once; his sister laughed knowing he was thrilled at the opportunity to house a war horse and gaze at the lance and shield.

I guess that's how boys are made, ready to go off and fight for a cause, kill or be killed; such a waste. Maybe there will always be wars. The young woman shook her head and her face wore a frown.

***

The young warrior slept through the night and awoke late the next day. His eyes opened and he focused on the sight of the slim maiden. Watching his hostess cooking over the fire, he was captivated by the golden locks that flowed like a waterfall down her back. His heart came alive at the sight of her.

He watched the young boy come in from playing with his shield and sword, pretending to be a great knight. He smiled at the youngster. The boy removed his coat and hat and stomped the mud off his boots.

Noticing the knight was awake, he went over and sat next to him. The boy asked the soldier, "Where are you going?"

The warrior smiled at the boy's interest in him. He remembered his innocent longing for adventure and faraway lands during his youth. "What is your name, boy?"

"Paul," the boy answered.

The man heaved a sigh. His face tightened and wrinkled in thought. "I have been to the north coast to fight the English."

The knight noticed the girl's eyebrows raise and she turned to face him. He looked into the deepest blue eyes he ever beheld and smiled. "You are wondering who I am. The mistress of the house should certainly know of who is her guest. I am John, of Rheims, second son of the Duke of Rheims. Now allow me to ask my most beautiful hostess her name."

The woman blushed beet red and was visibly shaken. She could not find words.

Her brother answered for her. "That's Julie, my sister."

Julie blushed even a shade darker. She bowed low to the ground and signaled to her brother to do the same.

"My lord, how may I please you?" She asked humbly.

"Arise my lady, and call me John, you please me with your beauty and your bread. I will see that you are rewarded for

your troubles," the young nobleman replied. "If you will allow, I would like some tea when it is ready, and the smell of the baguette waters my mouth."

Tea and bread were served by Julie, who became quite shy and quiet in the presence of the young nobleman. John thought this shyness added to her innocent beauty. He took her hand.

"Do not become withdrawn, your voice is much too sweet not to be heard. Come sit with me by the fire."

The three sat by the fire as the cold wind blew outside. Paul asked John questions about the war. John wanted to answer, but hesitated because a short answer would be incomplete. Finally, seeing that Julie too seemed interested, John agreed to talk about his misadventure.

"Peter, my lifelong friend, and I had just returned from a week-long hunting trip and we were in high spirits. Two bucks sat carved on our supply horse, our crossbows had proved their match. Saturday would be Peter's twenty-first birthday and there would be quite a feast."

"My older brother, Louis, greeted us with a smile and a laugh. He was always happy and robust. I used to think he never had a care in the world. Being the Duke's eldest, he was groomed for the position he would inherit. He was not the student I was, his math poor and he never learned Latin. Women and sport were always his first love. This love was repaid in kind, he was never lacking at either."

"Rich news brother," Louis announced, with a sparkle in his eyes. "The English have come again. This time we will drive those barbarians into the sea."

"Peter and I looked at each other with open mouths. So, we were to be at war. Oh, how lucky to be old enough to go and show our valor and courage, we thought."

"Great excitement had taken over our castle. Visitors from all points of France came and left with messages and news. Battle gear was hastily constructed. Our armaments were repaired, and shields were painted. It seemed the world was never so alive with excitement."

"Peter and I would talk loudly of how we would personally unseat King Henry of England and claim a great ransom for our Duchy and Kingdom. At night I would not be so brave and sleep came slowly.

"Saturday came and Peter's birthday arrived. A banquet was ordered by my father, who loved Peter like a son. Peter had lost his parents to the Plague and my father brought him into our house to be my youthful mate."

"Everyone was happy and excited. The women never looked so beautiful, decorated in the new arrivals from Paris. Venison, game hen, and sweet rolls were laid before us to the delight of our pallets."

"After dinner my father became serious and called all the knights of the castle together. Louis, Peter and I sat in a row on the right of father. The Duchess sat on his left."

"I have received word from the Duke of Orleans. The King has outlawed the Duke of Burgundy, John the Fearless. Burgundy has sided with the English. It is a deep blow to our kingdom. Our king has ordered us to march to join him. Monday we shall depart... I shall see you in church tomorrow gentleman. Now we shall drink and be merry! To Peter on his birthday."

"Peter stood. 'To our most noble duke.'"

"I felt my blood surge with excitement. Monday would not come soon enough for me. I rose 'To Charles, King of the French, we shall drive the English into the sea!'"

"Mother cried when we left on that Monday morning at dawn.

"Your mother is said to be the one of the most beautiful women in France," Julie interrupted.

"Ah my mother, I've heard people say she is beautiful but she is my mother, so she is special to me. When I was small, and I did wrong, the look in my mother's eyes would send me to my chamber in shame and I would cry."

"Well, what happened after you departed?" Paul asked impatiently.

"That is all for tonight, Julie quickly interjected, "it is well past the time for you to go to bed."

"Oh, Julie, I'm not tired," Paul begged.

"To bed!" she demanded.

Paul pouted like he had just lost his best friend. He crawled over to his straw bed and drew his feather quilt over him. Julie, acting more like a mother than a sister, tucked him in and kissed him goodnight. She blessed him and turned to see the young nobleman watching intently. Her face turned red and she felt drawn to her guest.

"You are a very good mother to him," John said.

She walked over to the fire and fed it another log. Flame flew and heat rose to consume its new captive as a spider might jump on a fly caught in its web. Embers hid the blush in Julie's face.

John touched her hand and she turned to him. Eyes met and locked his brown eyes to her blue. They could see each other's reflections in their eyes as the fire glowed. The embrace of their eyes was intense. Finally, Julie looked away.

"The first flowers of spring would look dull next to your beauty," John said, "Am I so unattractive that you must turn away?"

"Oh Sire, no!" Julie responded, "You are truly as fine a man as I ever set eyes upon. But the way you gaze at me makes me humble and blush."

"Come take my hand," he said.

Julie sat next to John and took his blistered and battered hand into her soft palm. He noticed her hands were cold while his were finally warm. He gazed at the peasant, her blond clashing with his dark locks. She made him feel whole and he could not resist his attraction to her.

John's lips brushed hers, and sparks flew. An embrace, a kiss, a touch, a wish drove them to an exciting new world. The storm raged outside, the fire blazed in the wall stones, and energy exploded into a passion between the two strangers. They made love. When the excitement calmed, Julie cried in John's arms.

"I love you," he said calmly.

"How could you love me? I am but a peasant. Now I am damaged goods and a sinner and you are the son of a duke," Julie said through her tears.

"You are a wonder of the world," he answered the young woman. "In all my life I could never hope to find such peace I have just realized with you."

Julie took his hand and kissed it. A second time they made love. This time the passions were quieter, and sincerer, like a cool breeze on a summer's day.

They fell asleep in each other's arms. Morning came to the world. The storm had subsided and a light drizzle fell. John helped with the chores and did much of the heavy work that had been neglected for lack of a man in the house. The three worked hard all day. Evening came and Julie began cooking dinner.

Dinner consisted of beans and bread, both fresh off the hot fire. The three gathered around the fire after dinner and Paul begged John to continue telling his story.

John started, "We rode early that morning. All of us were very excited about the upcoming battle and new adventure.

Five hundred proud knights of Rheims rode double file attended by their squires."

"My father, the duke, on his white horse led the way with my brother at his side. Our house's symbol of the silver fox was held brightly behind them. Peter and I were second in the company."

"Have you seen a nobler army," Peter said, "surely we could take on all of England."

"I readily agreed and we laughed and boasted as we followed the road along the Oise River, toward the Seine and Paris. Paris how grand, church spires that reached up toward the heavens and the clunk, clunk of your horse on the cobblestone streets. Bravely, nobly we rode through the wide avenues, sitting high in our saddles. Women of Paris waved from their windows. The young boys greeted us with cheers from every corner. We rode on to the palace of the king."

"I was truly thrilled, to see the King of France. The duke, my father, had met and counseled with the king's great father, Charles V. Under Charles, the kingdom was well united. He ruled well, order reigned. Most of the land conquered by the English King Edward III had been restored to French rule. But

Charles had died; his son was now the king, Charles VI. None of our family had met him. Rumor had it that he was insane."

"It was afternoon when we arrived at the palace. The Duke of Orleans personally greeted our party. The palace had swelled with people, as a river might swell with water after a great rain. Men in arms were everywhere."

"Welcome fine gentlemen!" Charles, Duke of Orleans greeted us, "Quarters will be provided for your army tonight in the city. Come Rheims and bring your sons, the king awaits."

"I said a quick goodbye to Peter and rushed to join my father and Louis."

"News is not all good my friends," Orleans began, to our surprise. "The King is not well. He has not been of sound mind for almost a year. We will march for Rouen the second sunrise. I will command the army, while the King will stay in Paris. The Duke of Bourbon will be my chief of staff and you, Rheims, will be his second."

"We had been walking to the banquet hall. Much of the nobility of France was in the room. Our places were pointed out. There were four great tables clothed in white. Benches ran along the sides of each. At the head of the first table there were two thrones, for the King and the Queen. Father was invited to sit at the first table, while Louis and I retreated to the third. We sat and engaged in conversation."

"Trumpets blared, 'Gentlemen the King,' a guard retorted. We all rose as Charles VI, King of France, entered the hall. The queen followed with the prince, Louis, but what attracted my immediate attention was the Princess Katherine. Such beauty, combined with grace, could only become the world once in a century. Helen of Troy and Cleopatra must have been such women. A blanket of light seemed to radiate from her white dress and pale skin."

"Henry of England, that villain of villains, now threatened to steal her from this court, and demand that she be his bride. Never! I thought."

"The King of France was boisterous and loud. He laughed loudly, and then retreated to periods of silence. So, our King was insane, I thought, at a period when we need him most. I felt disgusted with this man."

"Dinner was delicious, roast duck with nut bread and stuffing prepared by France's finest chefs. My gaze moved from the King to the Princess, from disappointment to wonder. My brother too, was infatuated with Katherine, as were all the men."

"The next day was spent in conference. Older knights who had fought the English before gave recommendations. A very heavy armor had been constructed to stop arrows of the English longbows. Crossbowmen were picked from Paris and outlying areas. Excitement jolted through my body, and I slept poorly that night."

"At dawn we rode for Rouen to meet other troops there. Halfway through the day a messenger arrived. The English had landed."

"I sweltered under my heavy armor. The news seemed to make the hot summer day a little warmer. It was August 13th. Some say thirteen is unlucky. I believed our enemies would be the unlucky ones."

"It took two weeks to reach Rouen. Camp was set along the Seine. Our army was arriving slowly from the far parts of France. The heat in camp was extreme and our movements seemed in slow motion. Everyone was uncomfortably uneasy."

"The first week of September came and we were still not ready to move against the invaders. Word came that the garrison of Hardliner had been lost. Still Orleans was not ready to move. I was dismayed by his lack of action, for I was anxious to meet the enemy."

"The end of September came and all was ready. We broke camp and moved north. The heat had not broken and although uncomfortable to our troops, spies learned the English had lost many to sickness and would retreat. I hoped not; I wanted to show those barbarians what it meant to invade our noble France."

"Moving north, our army swelled to over 20,000 men, proud nobility, the flower of the French, supported by the best of the hunters with crossbow and men at arms."

"By evening, October 14 our army reached the Somme River near Agincourt. The English were on the other side. Camp was set and a council of war was called. We would wait for the English to attack. When father told me of our plans, I protested. 'Father we outnumber them three to one. Surely victory will be ours if we attack.'"

"'Let us show them our lances!'" Louis agreed.

"'No, my good sons.Each day we grow stronger while the English grow weaker. Our supplies are good. The English grow hungry, and if they attack, how will they use their bow?'"

"Ten days we waited for the attack. It did not come. Then word was passed to prepare for battle. Finally, I thought with bliss, today was the day I would earn my manhood. As we prepared for battle, an angry wind came from the South.

Clouds thickened and it started to rain. Would the rain favor the English or our troops? I did not know."

"We were well organized. The Clugnet de Brabant and Count of Vendome headed the mounted troops. Louis was Vendome's captain. Peter and I were at his side."

"Henry had arranged his army in three divisions, which was traditional for the English. Each division was lined four deep, the last had trenched into the ground."

"Orleans and Bourbon headed our ground forces along with father. Our plan was to let the English attack. Forward they came. My blood rushed, I could hear my heart pound. Gritting my teeth, I found my hand gripping hard at my lance."

"Then the English stopped. We attacked, our crossbow men going first. The English long bows beat them back before they could get range and they broke ranks to flee. I didn't believe what happened next. Our ground forces cut off the crossbowmen's retreat and slaughtered them."

"Count Vendome shouted 'Forward,' and we went. My horse flew at full speed."

"The English bowmen let fly and the sky turned black. Arrows fell like rain, horses cried, men screamed. I put my shield up and the impact almost knocked me down. My brave mount bucked in panic. Somehow, I was not thrown as another arrow hit my shield. To the right of me I heard a scream. Turning I saw my sweet brother's face turn into a pool of blood."

"'Retreat!' cried Count Vendome as an arrow pierced his armor and entered his chest."

"'Let us be off,' I yelled to Peter, but he was already on the ground lying dead."

"The English then attacked. I fell behind our lines. The battle was over for me. I felt lost and in shock. Dismounting, my stomach let go and I was violently sick."

"The English were on top of our foot soldiers. Because of the heavy armor the French troops were wearing to ward off the longbow arrows, our men had trouble maneuvering in the mud. Charles, Duke of Orleans, fell trying to rally his men. The Duke of Bourbon took an arrow though the neck. The Duke of Rheims was then in command. Father died wielding his sword. I left after that moment and headed home. The battle of Agincourt was over."

The room had become silent. Julie and Paul fought back tears. The pain showed on the young knight's face and in the lines on his forehead.

Julie stroked John's hair and he closed his eyes and shivered. He screamed, "Oh God why?" and with a sigh he started to cry. John fell asleep in Julie's arms.

The rain stopped, as a new day started. Sunshine streamed down, shimmering on the silken surface. The tall black oak tree shook off the water dripping on its upper branches as a squirrel scurried up its side. The young knight looked out the front door as he dressed.

"Paul, be so kind as to get me my horse." John turned and walked over to where Julie was waking. He dropped to a knee at her bedside. "I must return home to assume the duties of my new title. I know we have just met and you are not of noble birth, but I am the new Duke of Rheims and I will send for you my love."

He kissed her deeply, knowing that the taste on his lips would have to last a long while. He left his armor, mounted his great horse and was off to the southeast. Julie and Paul stood outside and watched him ride away until he dropped off the horizon.

***

The young woman was sure he was gone; just an impossible interlude passing like wind and rain.

Days turned to nights and months passed. Spring approached and the old oak tree outside the inn budded and young leaves sprouted and grew. Julie and Paul were working in the garden planting vegetables to be served in meals at the Inn. Julie stabbed at the soil with a short stick making a row of small holes. Then she worked her way back, sowing the seeds, taking them out of a bag by her belt. Sweat dropped off her bonnet and into her muddy face as the sun reached higher in the sky.

Just before noon they heard the sound of horses coming up the road from the southeast. A coach appeared in the distance with an escort of knights. Julie could see a flag flying from the coach. She squinted into the sunlight at the pennant; it was a fox, the coat of arms of the Duke of Rheims!

The coach pulled up in front of the Inn. The coachman hopped down and opened the door. The Duke dressed in royal burgundy descended—Duke, John. He smiled looking down at her. Paul and Julie dropped to their knees and bowed.

"Arise my lady," John said, taking her hand. "I know I said I would send for you, but I could not wait to see you again."

He pulled her up from her knees. His arms surrounded her and his lips moved to hers. The kiss was long and deep.

The kingdom was about to gain a new duchess. The wind and the rain were gone from France, at least for a while.

It was spring, and for John, Julie and Paul, this fairy tale came true.

A True War Hero

How can a King lose a war and become one of the greatest heroes in World History? It is a story of great bravery a little bit of a myth, and circumstance.

King Christian X of Denmark was faced with two untenable decisions during World War II and history shows that his decision making leadership was infallible.

After the defeat of France and Belgium by the Germans in 1940 tiny Denmark faced the overwhelming Nazi forces as they invaded the country. After some token resistance, the Danish Government having consulted the King, decided to capitulate rather than put up an impossible defense and tremendous loss of life. Hitler, delighted by the surrender, called his occupation a protectorate and the Germans allowed the Danish Government to continue to rule from 1940 to 1942.

The Dictator deported Jews in other occupied countries but knowing that the Danish people supported their Jewish compatriots ignored the "Jewish problem" in Denmark. That policy changed in August of 1943. The Gestapo was ordered to start the evacuation of the Jews in Denmark.

Here is where the myth comes to play. Right before the Jewish New Year, the Jews were ordered to wear the Star of David to make identification easy for the Nazis. Supposedly King Christian wore the Star and the people of the nation followed his example and totally confused the occupational forces attempting the round up. Is the story true? Weeelll...maybe, maybe not...like George Washington and the cherry tree it's the symbolism that counts.

The Danish King and his people formed a Gandhi like resistance. The hid their follow citizens and embarked on a Dunkirk like evacuation of the Jewish people across the water to nearby unoccupied Sweden. Only about five hundred Jews were deported. Over seven thousand escaped right under the noses of the Nazis. This brave defiance probably made life more difficult for the Danish people. Yet they were the only country to make it a national policy to defy the German deportment of Jews.

Few people know about this amazing story today. It should be retold over and over. Hail King Christian X. As Jews say about the holocaust, never forget.

Are you tired of war stories?

Let's change the mood. Here is my true love story from my memoir **Not Quite Kosher:**

Finding Colleen

Many people ask me how Colleen and I met. I tell them she jumped out of the cake at a bachelor party.

"Really?" They would say.

"That's my story and I'm sticking to it."

Colleen tells people that I jumped out of the cake at a bachelorette party she attended.

So here is the boring truth. We met at a Chamber of Commerce mixer in Modesto. Neither of us had ever gone to a mixer before. It felt weird to be there, but making the most of the situation, I started talking to the woman next to me.

Her name was Hallie. During our conversation, I mentioned that I played tennis.

Hallie said, "My friend, Colleen, plays tennis."

Hearing her name, Colleen turned towards me. Was it love at first sight? No, not quite, but I was so attracted to her that I wasn't about to let her get away. We started talking and during our social intercourse, she told me she hated Modesto and was just here on a short assignment. She planned to return to San Francisco.

"I haven't even heard of a decent restaurant in this God-forsaken town."

I said, "Modesto is definitely not San Francisco but if you let me, I can take you to my favorite Italian restaurant. It's as good as some places I've eaten at in New York."

She didn't make it easy for me but she slipped me her card before she left.

"Call me about that restaurant," she said, with a twinkle in her dazzling green eyes.

Colleen told me later that she had a feeling from the start that I was going to be the man she married. She certainly didn't let me in on that little epiphany.

Thank goodness for Benny's. They really did have great homemade Italian food.

Hallie lied; Colleen couldn't play tennis.

When I met Colleen, I had been dating another woman who lived in Sacramento. Ursula was a nurse that I met through mutual friends.

I had already made a date to go camping with Ursula and her two delightful kids. I didn't want to stand them up, yet the whole time I was with them, I longed to be with Colleen. I realized that there had been a paradigm shift. There was no denying, I was in love with her. There was something special about her. Was it her sparkling green eyes when she smiled, her voice, the way she played with kids in a room full of adults? It was all of that. I just knew I wanted to be with her.

I came clean with Ursula. Needless to say, she was not a happy camper.

It was the fall of 1990 and Colleen was hosting her niece Ana who grew up in Spain. Colleen and I were spending more and more time together. Ana wondered who the heck I was and why I was monopolizing all of her aunt's time.

We went from casual to passionate quickly and couldn't keep our hands off each other. We would even make out in restaurant parking lots.

With Ana residing with her, Colleen would reluctantly go home. As soon as we got to our individual houses, we would call each other and whisper sweet nothings till the wee hours. Sparks flew out of our phones.

Three months into our relationship I took Colleen to her favorite Chinese restaurant in the Emeryville Marina on the water in the East Bay. She told me later she knew something was up because I was nervous and sweaty during the meal. She ordered Singapore Rice Stick noodles. I ordered General Tao's Chicken and asked her to marry me. I believe she was quite shocked.

"Will you give me some time to think about it?"

"Of course, take all the time you need."

She was quite quiet on the way home. She seemed to be contemplating; weighing her options. She never did tell me what she was thinking on that drive back to Modesto. She called me shortly after I dropped her off at her place.

"Yes, I will marry you," she said.

"You sure?"

She laughed, "Yeah, I guess you're stuck with me."

One funny postscript to the story took place a couple weeks later.

Colleen's best friends Dee and Dick had been traveling around the world during our romance and were totally incommunicado. When they landed in New York, they left a message to call them at their hotel.

Colleen and I were I huddled in a phone booth

Colleen excitedly relayed the news to Dee.

Dee insisted, "Put him on."

Her first words to me were, "Who the fuck *are* you?"

I fell in love with Dee immediately.

It's time to turn to my first love—sports

Growing up in New York the first team I rooted for was the all-powerful New York Yankees in the early '60s with Mantle and Maris. Being out on Long Island and a short subway ride away from Queens my interests turned to those lovable losers, the Mets. Then came super cool Broadway Joe and the Jets. After the Navy, I became a Bay Area sports fan, with our share of good and bad teams. But the following sports event stands alone in time and my mind.

Another excerpt from **Not Quite Kosher:**

Rock and Roll

It was baseball heaven for Bay Area fans, Giants verses A's, a Bay Bridge World Series. Tony La Russa's Bash-brothers vs Roger Craig's, Will "The Thrill" and Keven Mitchell. The upstart A's had taken the first two games at the Oakland Coliseum but game three moved to the Giants home, at windy old Candlestick Park.

I know it's lame to root for both teams, yet the Giants were my first love. But from Modesto, it was so much easier to get to the Coliseum. So, I had a partial season ticket plan for the brassy young A's. With Mark McGuire and Jose Canseco bashing tape measure bombs (we didn't know yet that they had been using performance enhancing drugs) and the classy handlebar-mustached closer, Dennis Eckersley slamming the door, Oakland's team was fun. Having met Will Clark the year earlier, my loyalties were truly torn.

For the third game, I arrived early at Mini's, claimed my seat at the bar and ordered a club soda. It was much too early to tackle a mixed drink or even a beer. World Series night games started before dinner on the left coast so the networks could garner the New York prime time audience. We didn't yet know how many lives would be saved getting rush hour traffic off the Bridge and the freeways before the game started.

Then the world shook. Even in Modesto, ninety miles east of the epicenter, the bar felt like a cabin-cruiser that had been hit by a huge wave. The TV behind the bar flickered then went to static scratching snow. The outrigger canoes shook from the ceiling rafters. Everyone looked at each other with eyes as big as saucers.

"Holy shit!" I mouthed silently.

I ran out to the car and tuned to KCBS, the all-news radio station; nothing. Then a women's frightened voice could be heard. "That must have been an earthquake." Slowly she gained her composure and started reporting. "Our building swayed intensely but everyone here at the station appears to be okay. USGS reports the epicenter to be just north of San Jose with a magnitude of 6.9 on the Richter scale." I turned the car off and went back into Mini's and ordered a Screwdriver, which seemed appropriate. It wasn't too early anymore.

The television came back to life, with Al Michaels a former Bay Area resident, doing the play by play of the Loma Prieta Earthquake; the canceled World Series game, suddenly unimportant and forgotten.

I watched with horror as he reported the Bay Bridge and Embarcadero Freeway collapses, then the Marina District fires.

We in California expect earthquakes, but just like people in Oklahoma who have often felt the wrath of tornadoes, dealing with the damage and death was not going to be easy. The greatest damage came where expected, land fill areas that were once part of San Francisco Bay.

The Series continued 10 days later with the A's sweeping the Giants. Never was a championship more of an anticlimax.

December 3, 2013

Goodbye to The Stick

Today the 49ers close out Candlestick Park. I can't remember who the Giants played the first time I visited that concrete monstrosity but soon I realized that Mark Twain was probably at this point of land when he made his claim that, "The coldest winter I ever spent was a summer in San Francisco."

The Mark Twain I have read loved baseball and the city. I think his ghost may have been sitting next to me watching McCovey uppercut a ball into the almost empty right field seats near me. I never did get the name of the gentleman who grabbed the ball and talked to me about Ty Cobb's racism and Babe Ruth's legend. The man sported a St. Louis stocking hat and also talked about the Mississippi, so maybe…nah.

That was just one of many *Windlestick* moments I spent in the home of both the Giants and 49ers for so many years. I became a San Francisco fan when I moved to the Bay Area in 1971.

There were the best of times, those five championships of the 49ers; and the worst of times, when I attend what was to be the Giant's last game in S.F. before moving to Tampa. Luckily that deal fell through.

I was not there in 1989 for the Bay Bridge World Series Game A's vs. Giants—when rock and roll at the ball park meant 6.9 on the Richter scale but I will never forget that famous "rainout." The stick survived the earthquake and a lot of people owe their lives to its resiliency.

So, when they blow up the joint this year I have mixed feelings. Goodbye Candlestick, and Mays, McCovey, Montana, Young, Clark (Will and Dwight) and Rice. Will I miss you? The answer is *blowin'* in the wind.

The San Francisco Giants were very good in the 50's and 60's with Willie Mays, Willie McCovey, Juan Marichal, Orlando Cepeda; then again in the 80's led by Will Clark but never good enough to win it all. The Giants toiled in the city by the bay for fifty years without winning a championship. Until...

The October Invasion

They came from the southwest first appearing in the summer of 2010. Some entomologists believed they were a mutated desert variety. By October of 2012 the large black ants infected the whole midwestern United States. It was discovered that they lay their eggs in riverbanks, or near water, and swarm into the cities in the cool of the evening. They were carnivorous, leaving nasty bites on warm blooded animals of the bird and mammal phyla, like some type of plague of biblical proportions.

The States of Michigan, Ohio and Missouri called out their best specialists and the militia. They fought back against the onslaught. Massive budgets were provided to the local combatants. Experts studied the insect's mode of operation extensively on film. The mutant strain of ants was beaten back and appeared to be defeated but like cockroaches they survived all attempts to wipe them out. They came back stronger than ever.

They swept though the city of Detroit, attacking even in the zoo, biting so furiously even big cats were left emaciated. Looking closely at the bugs you could see they had bright

orange mandibles. Finally, the entomologists realized they were not from the desert after all but from Northern California. They had been developed in a laboratory next to San Francisco Bay, combining South American with North American varieties. The ravaged Midwesterners finally realized what type of ant they were up against. They were the World Champion Gi-ants.

The Land of the Giants

I grew up in a magic land of **Giants,**
It had the tallest buildings in the world.
A lovely giant woman welcomed newcomers,
standing magnificent above the great harbor.

How I loved to watch those **Giants** play.

Of course, being **Giants,** they played ball *uptown,*
in the only place big enough, the *Polo Grounds.*
Their best player had a game so large
He had to reach down to catch a fly ball.

But the people stopped believing in **Giants,**
would not come to watch them play
or build them a glorious new home.

So, the **Giants** moved to a new magic land,
where the hills climb halfway to the stars
and trees grow so tall they blocked out the daytime sun
The people in this new land believed in the **Giants;**
built them a glorious new home.

I climbed the beanstalk and followed the Goliaths to the new land.

How I love to watch these **Giants** play.

The Bay Area boys of summer won three World Series in six years from 2010 to 2016. The 2014 team inspired these two poems:

Who That Foe From?

Fee fi foe fum, I smell the blood of a Royal?

What the he-ll is a roya-ll

From Webster: family of king or queen especially English

So, fee fi foe from-Queens, not Dodgers from Brooklyn?

Both blue, but Royal Blue?

Hard to get my knickers in a twist for Royal Blue

But it is the serious World Series, so

Fee fi foe fum, I smell the blue blood of an Englishman

Eat 'em up Giants

A Goodbye Too Soon

Dwight Clark, famous 49er is gone

to an end zone in the great beyond

victim of ALS, Lou Gehrig's Disease

blown away like a Candlestick breeze

He and his team captured Bay Area fans

when Montana's pass found his hands

Clark's Jordan-like jump and sure handed snatch

became a San Francisco legend known as *the catch*

Down went the dreaded Cowboys

discarded like childhood toys

on to win that first Super-bowl and the rest

Dwight and the 49ers proved they were best

So, let's pop the cork of Napa's best wine

And toast Dwight Clark's catch, so divine

Golden Record

Let us all lift a toast

to the team with the most

you would think it would be hard to relate

to the team Golden State

But in tee's that say: The City

they look oh so pretty

raining down threes

playing D like swarms of bees

with a game on the line

spicy Curry says. It's mine

the quickest shot in the west

shows why he is now the best

The shot goes in

Warriors have another win

three beats two every time

Splash Brother's shooting so sublime

The Bull's with MJ so great

but they were to resign to fate

to the new best team

playing hoops like a dream

The following is an excerpt from:

Roger Raintree's Seventh Grade Blues, A Young Adult Novel.   I was tutoring a young boy and wanted to write something he would enjoy reading:

The Runaway

Did you ever have a really bad day? You know, the kind where nothing goes right? So bad you want to run away? Well, last Wednesday was that kind a day for me.

Let me tell you; running away was not my best idea.

My name is Roger Raintree.

I live in Middletown, right in the middle of the good old U.S.A.

My favorite things are: baseball, good friends, pizza and now that I'm in the seventh grade, maybe even girls.

I go to Middletown Middle School in the middle of the suburbs of St. Louis, Missouri.

Wednesday morning, first thing when I got up, I had to go really bad, so I went. I was sitting there reading the sports scores when my older brother, 'Big Bird', yelled at me, "Roger, stop stinking up the bathroom. I need to get in there."

156

My brother's real name is Joseph or Joey. I'd tell you why everybody calls him 'Big Bird' but that's another story.

"Okay already. I'm just about done," I yelled back through the door. So, I finished my business, opened the door and he punched me hard in the arm.

"That's for stinking up the whole place."

"Mom, Joey hit me hard," I yelled down to her in the kitchen.

"Joey, stop hitting your brother," she called back. Like that's going to stop him.

Dad would be more helpful here. He is good at keeping the Big Bird away from me but he left early to commute to work in the city.

I jumped into most of my clothes but I didn't have a clean shirt cause I forgot to give my mom my laundry. I picked out the one that looked the cleanest and pulled it on, but I forgot to give it the underarm smell test. That would become a big problem.

Mom had a cold so her voice sounded funny. "Grab a peanut butter and jelly sandwich and drink your milk."

"Yuck, Mom, not chunky peanut butter, you know I hate chunky."

"Yes, I know, but Joey likes chunky and it's his turn," she says.

From her voice I could tell her nose was stuffy and she wasn't feeling good but I couldn't help myself. Mockingly I said, "It's chunky Big Turds' turn, the stupid big butthead."

She gave me one of her killer looks and I stopped real fast. Mom is a high school teacher and she could say more with one look than most people could say with a whole speech.

I noticed in the mirror my hair was sticking up wildly. I tried the comb, then the brush but I couldn't get it right. Finally, I gave up, shrugged my shoulders. I guess it's also going to be a bad hair day.

I was late for the bus so I sprinted fifty yards and hopped on just before it left. I was already sweaty so I picked an empty seat.

The bus pulled into the next stop. Then on that day, of all days, Sharon, just about the cutest girl in school, slid into the seat next to me.

She looked up, then crinkled her pretty nose and shouted, "Oh my God Roger, you smell so bad. It's like something died in your shirt." She grabbed her book bag and ran to another seat.

That's it, I thought. I'm totally messed up. I can never ever go to school again.

I zoomed to the front to get off the bus but evil driver, Miss Evans, the twin of Oz's Wicked Witch of the West, yelled,

"Sit down Roger!"

Ignoring her, I moved my body toward the door. My eyes had misted up but I can't cry in front of everyone. I felt it slowly moving down my face like a slug, the wet tear. Miss Evans repeated, "Roger you must sit down now!"

The next thing I knew I was pounding on the door. "Let me out, let me out, LET ME OUT!"

Wicked Witch pulled over and the door to freedom opened. I jumped out and heard, "Bus 5 to base, we have a problem."

I sprinted away, realizing I was in big trouble and headed straight home.

I felt safe at my house for the moment cause no one was home. I changed the nasty shirt, finally finding a clean one that I never wear cause it's got the stupid Chicago Cubs on it.

I grabbed all my money, $6.77, two granola bars and a water, tossed them into my pack and I was off.

To where? I didn't know.

I tried to calm down while moving up the street. After fifteen minutes the granola bars were gone and I found myself in front of the mall.

I went in, but on a weekday morning it was dull, empty, and lifeless. I entered a shop and saw some cool stuff but I had little money to spend.

In the Apple computer store, the security guard's eyes followed me like I was a common thief.

I realized I was getting hungry as I passed the empty food court with their overpriced crappy stuff and walked out the exit.

Drifting north away from the mall, school and neighborhood, I wanted to be away from my usual turf. Why? I didn't know. It seemed like a good idea at the time.

I was hiking by the side of the highway along an empty sidewalk when I noticed the man out of the corner of my eye.

I remembered that he had left the mall right behind me. Then he wandered out of my sight. Re-appearing, he was moving up on me fast and he gave me the creeps. You know how some people make you nervous just looking at them? Well this guy was one of those, times five.

He had a straggly beard, olive-green army fatigues, a plain black ball cap and those weird mirrored sunglasses where you can't see a person's eyes. I walked faster, but he still gained on me...oh my, I thought I saw a knife in his hand.

I was frightened, like totally scared. I thought maybe I should make a run for it when I saw the diner, like an oasis in the desert. Our family ate there often. I sprinted to the door and crashed through like I was coming around third and the catcher was blocking home plate. I could almost hear the umpire yell; Safe!

I relaxed as the smell of pizza, pasta, fried chicken, and cheeseburgers overwhelmed my senses and my mouth watered. I slid into an empty booth. The whole place looked deserted. I figured it must have been after breakfast and before lunch.

A pretty waitress with short dark hair was watching me as I counted my money; while I glanced longingly at the menu. She was young but old, like twenty-five, a real grown up woman. She walked over and I saw her name tag said Becky.

Her face smiled at me with warm brown eyes. "Can I get you something sweetie?"

I looked away from Becky to my money and said, "I'll just have a Coke."

She slid her order pad and pen in her vest pocket and said, "I'll be right back."

I tried to think. What could I do now? I had almost no money and that creep might still be out there. I couldn't go home cause I'm in so much trouble.

Becky brought my Coke and a big plate of French fries. "Don't worry, the fries are on me." Then she looked at me with knowing eyes and asked, "Are you having a bad day?"

I felt surprise and tried to put a smile on my face. "Thanks," came out of my mouth but I wanted to say more.

"Is it okay if I sit a second?" she asked.

I nodded.

As she sat, she asked,

"What's your name?"

After I told her, she said again,

"Roger, are you having a bad day?"

"How did you know?" I asked.

"Well, we all have bad days."

"You have 'em?"

"Sure," she said

I could smell her perfume. It smelled real good, like pretty flowers. You know, the kind that dad would bring home for mom.

She asked me, "Did you run away?"

Surprised, I asked, "Are you one of them psycho-people?"

She gave me a funny look; then giggled. "You mean psychic. No, I'm just concerned. I ran away once, about when I was your age; about thirteen, right?"

"Twelve-and- a-half. You really ran away?"

"Yes, I did."

"Are you a mom?"

"No, I'm working here part-time while I'm going to college. I'm still very single."

"Oh," I said. It was quiet for a minute. She didn't say anything, just waited for me. Finally, I said, "What did you do after you ran away?"

"When I came to my senses, I went home."

I sighed. "I can't go home. I'm in too much trouble. Mom and Dad are going to kill me."

"What in the world did you do that was so horrible?"

I told her all about what happened on the bus.

She smiled; then laughed. "Is that all? Okay, let me tell you two little secrets. First of all, that girl Sharon wouldn't have sat next to you if she didn't like you. Wear some clean clothes from now on. She'll come around."

"Second, when you have a bad day, don't run away. Tell your mom or dad. They will understand. They have bad days too."

I thought about what she said and realized she was probably right. "How did you get so smart?"

Her face lit up with a laugh. "I don't know, maybe it's from being in college. Tell you what; give me your mom'phone number. I'll call her for you. You know; to break the ice."

"Really?"

"Sure."

I tapped the number on my cell phone and gave it to her. She took it and walked behind the counter. I could see her talking for a while and then she came back and gave me the phone.

"Your dad's coming. Your mom said to bring you a cheeseburger. Is that okay?"

"Sure, thanks." I was still a little worried about *the creep* who scared me before I came into the diner. I told Becky about him and she told her manager. The police took him to jail the next day, but that's another story.

About a half-hour later, I was just finishing the cheeseburger and licking my fingers when my dad came in. He sat down next to me and ruffled my hair. "So, I hear you're having a bad day."

"Yeah; sorry Dad. I hope I didn't mess things up for you at work."

"No, it's fine son. Mom called me and I was happy to come get you. I just took a long lunch and can finish my work at home."

"You know, when you have a bad day, Mom and I feel bad for you."

"Really?"

"Yes, absolutely."

I thought about it; then broke into a grin.

"Dad, would you do something for me?" I gave him all the money I had.

"Will you give this to my waitress for a tip?" With a laugh, he rubbed my hair again.

"Don't worry, I took care of the bill and gave her a really big tip. I think you should take this money, go over and give it to her yourself."

So, I scooted over and gave Becky the money. She bent down and kissed me on the cheek then gave me a big hug.

"Thanks," I said, "you're the best waitress ever."

She looked at me, then at my dad and said, "Why is it that all the good men are either too young or too old?" She giggled, brown eyes twinkling.

Dad grabbed my hand. We walked out of the restaurant together.

So, I don't really recommend running away when you have a bad day.

It's funny, cause I saw Becky the very next day...but that's another story.

Teri Kerry--"Roger Raintree is a little bit of Tom Sayer and a little bit of Huckleberry Finn."

I was due to have Surgery. a Deep Brain Stimulus unit placed in my head to help control my Parkinson's shaking when the idea came to me to create a hero who derived his power from a displaced unit in his head. So, into the night came the Black Knight. The world got a new superhero and I got DBS.

Excerpt from **Black Knight of Berkeley:**

Chapter 1   Man in Shadows

He was invisible, just another shadow in the darkness, dressed head-to-toe in black, hiding, waiting for the dream to reappear. He'd seen it, all too clearly, in his dream.

Were they dreams or nightmares?

He knew this was the place it would happen.

One hour from midnight he'd seen her emerge from the BART station. She walked quickly, heels clicking on the sidewalk. Her assailant was now behind her, just feet away, the dark skin of both almost invisible in the blackness of night.

In another moment the knife would be at her throat. The movement was quick, never leaving the shadows. His cane came down on the back of the assailant's neck. The man fell, knife clanging bell-like on the sidewalk. She saw his shadow moving quickly away, and knew he had saved her.

"Who are you?"

She heard his doppler voice. "I am the black of night."

Kathy Linden didn't stop running until she was safe in her apartment. Then she called 911. Berkeley Police found an unconscious man and his knife on the Shattuck Street sidewalk.

The assault was recorded on the back pages of the **Chronicle** and the end of the local newscasts.

She called him *The Black Knight*. In his dream, her death and her blood spilled across the front pages of the newspaper and the beginning of the local newscasts.

Past-Times

Time rolls right along
sometimes singing our songs

But time reminds us to pay the piper
years pass making our bodies riper

Now that I've reached age sixty-eight
with Parkinson's I don't always feel so great

I remember being young and spry
senior year, 1968, at South High

That last summer driving to Long Beach
pretty girls in bikini's almost in reach

I do remember kissing a few
after drinking too many brews

At parties with friends
I thought fun would never end

But by that fall I'd be in the Navy
so those times began to get hazy

Childhood days became dreams far away
in California I would live, work and play

Have new friends, son Sam to hold,
wonderful wife, with whom to grow old

Climate change is causing Northern California to be drier.

Drought conditions in the summer months were normal and so were fires. In the last few years winter rains have been scarce causing fire season to last year round and become much more dangerous. 2017 was particularly bad for Napa and Sonoma Counties, otherwise known as Wine Country.

Wine Country Fires Autumn 2017

Fires snaked wide paths

through our Garden of Eden

driven by bone dry Diablo Winds

blowing, blasting through houses on

hillsides of redwood forests,

across acres of the fruit of the vines,

devouring whole neighborhoods.

Infernos sent residents on an exodus of evacuation

fleeing like the Israelites from Pharaoh's army.

Those spared from the ungodly wrath,

could only pray for friends and neighbors

left destitute by destruction

and felt the guilt of survival.

MOTHER NATURE'S PLAN
November 2017

Fires in the Redwood Empire
are as natural as fog on S.F. Bay.
Pacific high-pressure plants
over Nor-Cal sending storms away,
causing summer drought.
Vegetation dries out
just waiting for a spark.
Flames explode burning
dry grasses and low timber.
Redwoods, evolved in this clime,
with thick smoldering bark
and green needle crowns
in the heavens above fiery hells,
survive and turn fog into raindrops
quenching big trees thirst.
Autumn comes and high pressure
moves south for the winter
like snowbirds to Florida.
Rain returns, redwood cones
opened by summer inferno
drop seeds, baby redwoods

grow in the ashes.

Brown and scarred black hills,

magically turn green.

Deer prance and mountain lions stroll

coyotes howl, life goes on....

Thicker than Smoke October 22, 2017

This morning as Rue and I walked the mile on the trail through vineyards from the library to the bone-dry Napa River, I realized just how lucky we were. Smokey haze had been replaced with clean air for the first time since the Sunday night when our fiery ordeal started. Overnight, light moist ocean breezes blew the evil air out of the valley. Puffy cumulus clouds dotted the blue sunshiny sky. Up north over Mount St. Helena darker stratus clouds promised rain. Our little town of St. Helena appears to have been spared.

In the midst of all the devastation I want to share two happy stories. Last Tuesday, Colleen, our friend Mary, Rue and I evacuated to San Francisco. We stopped for lunch on Clement Street still weighing our options as to which family or friends to impose ourselves upon. After eating, with Colleen and Mary still conversing, I took Rue outside and came upon a couple smooching. I asked, "Excuse me, do you two know each other?"

The lady laughingly said, "Yeah... I think so."

That started a conversation where I explained that we had come down from the fire. They left wishing me luck. A few minutes later the women came back and gave me her number and invited us to stay at their unoccupied apartment in Berkeley. While I told her we had other options, I was taken aback by their generosity. "Thank you so much," was all I could say.

Last night we went out for dinner at "Market" in downtown St Helena. In the back were a large group of tables filled with firefighters from San Diego that the restaurant had been feeding all week. This was their last night after ten days of twelve-hour shifts. As they stood to leave after taking pictures, the patrons and staff gave them a standing ovation. A multitude of firefighters had saved our town.

There was a sign in the window that said, "The love is thicker than the smoke."

Indeed.

Assignment: Write a flash fiction piece or poem from the point of view of a person of the opposite sex.

Another West Side Story

I had just graduated from Columbia with a degree in English Literature. I was staying in the New York Hilton on west 54th street, having just seen the play *West Side Story* with my parents. It was their graduation present, along with the stay at the hotel. I had one more night in the big city before I turned back into Cinderella, going home to Albany. My parents left an hour earlier; their car full of things from my dorm room. I was nursing a drink and smoking a cigarette in the bar feeling a little sorry for myself, not having met Prince Charming at college. What does one do with a degree in English Lit? Did I really want to teach nouns and verbs to a bunch of pimply teenagers?

Then if by magic he walked into the bar and sat next to me. "I'll have a scotch neat," He said to the bartender.

Paul Newman was sitting next to me! He was shorter than I expected but the man had to have the bluest eyes I had ever seen. He turned to me and smiled. I almost melted.

"I don't suppose I could bum one of those from you. I'm trying to quit, but it's hard."

"Sure Mr. Newman." I held out the pack trying to keep my hand from shaking.

"Please call me Paul and let me buy you one of those…what are you drinking?" He nodded to the bartender.

"A Manhattan."

He laughed. "How appropriate."

I couldn't help myself, I gushed. "Mr. Newman, I loved you in *Butch Cassidy and the Sundance Kid.*"

"Please call me Paul."

"Yes Mr…Paul, I really did like it. You and Mr. Redford were amazing. Are you friends like that when you're not doing a movie?"

"Friendly enough. He actually is a great guy. But we don't get together very often. We both are on the road making movies. He likes to ski and I like to race cars."

"Are you in town making a movie?" I asked trying to keep his attention.

"No, doing a fund raising event for the Democratic Party." He looked at his watch." I'd like to talk to you some more, you seem very nice, but I've got to run." Paul finished his drink, peeled off a twenty and left it on the bar. He thanked me for the cigarette and stood up.

"Paul, will you sign this for me, no one will believe..."

"Sure, who do I make it out to?"

"Cathy."

He wrote something on my *West Side Story* program, handed it to me and sauntered away like a cowboy in a western movie. I looked at the program.

To Cathy,

Thanks for the smoke, pretty lady

Paul Newman.

I saved that program of *West Side Story*. *Butch Cassidy and the Sundance Kid* is still one of my favorite movies. Every time I buy salad dressing, I think of the night Paul Newman called me a pretty lady and bought me a drink

A Different View

I have a confession to make; I hated the Word Trade Centers. That was before 9-11 when the terrorists crashed in to them and killed all those innocent people, turning the grounds into an American shrine. They also ruined my perfectly good joke about the buildings. I used to say, "Those buildings look like the boxes the Empire State and Chrysler Buildings came in." The joke is no longer apropos and is no longer funny.

Those bastards also stole that day from us and made it a day of national mourning. With all due respect to the dead and their loved ones, I say we take back that day. I know a boy who was born on 9-11; should he never celebrate on his special day?

Has enough time passed for some gallows humor?

Well here goes.

Maybe those guys were just really bad pilots.

Actually, they were really—really bad pilots and were aiming for the Chrysler and Empire State Buildings.

They originally planned the attack for December 7th but heard it was already taken. (Pearl Harbor Day)

When a reporter found one of the mothers of one of terrorists he asked her, "Did you believe he would go to heaven with 72 virgins? She answered, "If I knew he would grow up to like virgins so much I would have stayed one."

Life is short, all days need a little humor.

More bad humor:

A young man took his seat on a plane, when the most beautiful woman he had ever seen sits down next to him. After the plane takes off the two engage in conversation.

"I hope you don't mind me asking but I find you amazingly attractive. After we land would you sleep with me for a million dollars?"

The woman goes over the offer in her mind. A million bucks could set me up for life and the guy is kind of cute.

"Yes," she says, "I will."

"How about for $20?"

"Are you crazy? What kind of girl do you think I am?"

"We already established that, now we're just dickering on the price."

I love this joke. It implies everyone has his/her price.

Classic Classical Rock

If Beethoven were alive today

would he still write

in classical mode?

I think not.

What would he write?

Rock? Blues? Jazz? Punk? Rap?

Or would the greatest musician ever

find something totally unique?

Maybe he would write

an electric fifth symphony

he on piano

rocking it with Clapton on guitar.

Whatever-- please buy me a ticket.

Jefferson's Confession

What was my worst sin?

I became what I rebelled against.

I rebelled against the absolute power of a king

But I was elected to become a king

I rebelled against

the power of the feudal government

and George Washington

but used that power

like I was a king

I rebelled against Hamilton's national bank

but kept it and used it

to buy Louisiana

from that anti-rebel, rebel Napoleon

like I was a king

the rebel believed all men should be free

but I kept men as slaves

like I was a king

I loved a slave and she bore my children

but they were my bastards

like I was a king

I built a palace at Monticello

like I was a king

So, was I the rebel or the anti-rebel

Yes, I confess I guess.

July 4, 2018

I've recently joined a Readers Theater Ensemble. So, I find myself writing some short play scripts.

Here are two examples:

Driving Her Crazy

By Nathaniel R. Winters

Characters some scripts

Jan 65-year old woman

Sue 66-year old woman

Don 66-year-old man, Jan's husband

Scene I: At the mall

Friends Jan and Sue are shopping.

Sue

How did you get here?

Jan

My grandson wanted to use the car. So, he dropped me off.

Sue

Your grandson is driving now. Wow that is so cool. I can remember picking him up for soccer practice when he was just a little tike. I have my car in the parking lot. Do you want a ride home with me? We can stop at the new bakery on the way.

Jan

Sure, a ride would be nice. I've been meaning to stop and try their fresh made bread. I hear it's delicious.

Sue

Now, where is the car? I always park it here.

Jan

Are you sure?

Sue

Oh no! It's finally happened.

Jan

What?

Sue

I left my keys in the car and it's been stolen. My husband has warned me so many times, "Don't leave your keys in he car, it will get stolen." He says, "If your head weren't attached you'd forget to put it on in the morning." I'm not sure which is worse; getting the car taken or having to tell Don he was right.

Jan

Well, you had better call the police.

(Sue pulls out her cell-phone}

Sue

Hello, I need to report a stolen car. (Pause)

Sue Davenport   (Pause)

A 2017 Honda SUV, Blue (Pause)

License number? I'm not sure. Let me call my husband and I'll get back to you. (Pause)

Yes, Thanks.

Now the hard part, telling Don he was right.

Hello, Don, I hate to tell you this, our car was stolen.

                    Don

Honey, I dropped you off at the mall two hours ago and I'm in our car right now.

                    Sue

Oh...Well then can you pick me up?

                    Don

I'd love to honey but first I have to convince this cop that just pulled me over that I didn't steal our car.

Ghosts of Abbott and Costello

go to a rock and roll show

Abbott

I never went to one of these, which band plays first

Costello

The Who

Abbott

Who?

Costello

That's right.

Abbott

What's right? Who's on first?

Costello

Exactly.

Abbott

So exactly plays first?

Costello

No Who plays first.

Abbott

That's what I'm asking you, who plays first?

Costello

Correct, Who plays first.

Abbott

Noooooo! Let' try again. Who plays first?

Costello

That right.

Abbott

Okay let's try this. Who plays second?

Costello

No, Who plays first. Guess Who plays second.

Abbott

Now you want me to guess who is playing second. Who is on first?

Costello

That is right.

Abbott

What is right?

Costello

Who is on first and Guess Who is playing second.

Abbott

That is what I'm asking you, who is playing second?

Costello

No, Who plays first. Guess Who plays second.

Abbott

I don't want to guess who's on second. Let me ask you does a band play third?

Costello

Yes.

Abbott

Yes, tell me the band playing third.

Costello

Yes.

Abbott

Who play first. Guess Who plays second and Yes third?

Costello

Correct.

Abbott

How can that be correct? I don't know what I just said. Tell you what let's get out of here and go back to being gratefully dead.

Costello

No, the Dead play fourth.

Abbott

Now you're telling me ghosts play rock music.

Costello

Not ghosts. The Grateful Dead.

Abbott

Who's dead?

Costello

No, Who's first, the Dead play fourth.

Abbott

Let's haunt a baseball game. This all seems Déjà vu.

Costello

Déjà vu? We missed them they played yesterday.

I hope you don't mind
If I do a few rhymes:

Once upon a time
There was a young knight

who got into a terrible fight

jousting with his lady all night

they made up before sun up

and made love all morn

just nine months later

a new knight was born

        ***

There was a girl named Alice

who wanted to live in a palace

she took LSD instead

which played with her head

followed bunny down his hole

now works at Mad Hatter Bar

slinging beers and singing solo.

***

There once was a guy name Nate

who took an Irish lass on a date

they had so much fun

he knew she was the one

they found each other so dear

been married for twenty-six years.

There it is, this third little limerick, my happy ending.

It is about me and my lovely wife Colleen,

my favorite heavenly body.

Alfred Hitchcock said "There would be no happy endings,
unless you know when to end the story."

So, I'll end this book here.

The books of Nathaniel Robert (Bob) Winters

Something for everyone:

Roger Raintree's 7th Grade Blues   Young adult:

A modern early teen adventure with relevant lessons to be learned in each chapter

Finding Shelter from the Cold   Young Adult and adults that have a love of dogs: — Ice age fictional story about wolves becoming dogs. Its source was an ABC nature film using DNA evidence. Will remind the reader of Jack London's Call of the Wild

Adult Novels: *The Adventures of the Omaha Kid-*

Romance, adventure, sports, triumph and tragedy

Penngrove Ponderosa- Story of Sonoma State students in the early 70's—sex, drugs with the shadow of Vietnam in the background

Sci-fi: *Past the Future*—Space ships, baby factories, Clones, Time machines just for starters. Will Dave save the world?

Black Knight of Berkeley—Hero Murder Mystery

Poetry and short stories:

The Poet I Didn't Know and

Another Revolution

Fictionalized biography:

Rumors about my Father,

No Place for a Wallflower

Legend of Heath Angelo

Not Quite Kosher-Memoir

Heavenly Bodies and other Diversions- Stories, poems

About the Author:

Nathaniel Robert "Bob" Winters joined the Navy from NYC. The Vietnam Veteran earned his BA in history from Sonoma State College and a Master's of Education from CSU Stanislaus. The retired teacher has written and published 12 books appealing to a variety of age groups. His prose and poetry have won awards and can be found published in many anthologies and magazines. Bob lives with his wife, son and dog in the Napa Valley. Despite having Parkinson's disease, he writes almost every day.

Made in the USA
San Bernardino, CA
13 May 2019